Also by Peggy Heinkel-Wolfe
See Sam Run: a mother's memoir of autism

Also by Shahla Ala'i-Rosales
 (with Linda A. LeBlanc and Tyra P. Sellers)
Building and Sustaining Meaningful and Effective Relationships
 as a Supervisor and Mentor

Responsible and Responsive Parenting in Autism:
 Between Now and Dreams

Copyright © 2024, 2021 Shahla Ala'i-Rosales and
 Peggy Heinkel-Wolfe

Second edition published by:
 Love and Science Publishing
 Denton, Texas 76201
 Betweennowanddreams.com

All rights reserved. Permission is granted for the user to photocopy limited excerpts for instructional use only (not for resale or other commercial use). No other part of the material protected by this copyright notice may be reproduced or used in any form or by any means, electronic or mechanical, including photocopying and recording or by any information storage and retrieval system without prior written permission by the copyright owners.

Cover painted by Dena Abbas Pritchett
ISBN Number: 979-8-9914453-0-6
Library of Congress Number: 2024946543

Responsible and Responsive Parenting in Autism: Between Now and Dreams

Shahla Ala'i-Rosales and Peggy Heinkel-Wolfe

This book is dedicated to our parents, who taught us our first lessons about humanity, responsibility, and the power of love and science; and to our children, who continue to inspire us to be responsive.

Contents

Getting Started   9

Part One: The Power of Learning   20
    In the Beginning   21
    Science for Sale   26
    A Science of Love and Change   29
    Evidence-Based Treatment   36
    Unexpected Places to Find Wisdom   43
    Sustainability   47
    Attitude Matters   52
    Shifting Toward Halcyon Attitudes   55
    Change is Intentional   57
    Learning to Learn   64

Part Two: The Power of Connecting   73
    Reciprocity Fosters Connections   74
    Building Strength and Resilience   78
    Learning From Each Other   82
    Seeing Around Our Blind Spots   84
    Being an Equal Among Professionals   87
    Sharing Wisdom and Responsibility   92
    In the Family   98
    Danger Signs and Exit Strategies   101
    Scouting for Places of Connection   104
    Connecting with Intention   108

Part Three: The Power of Loving   110
   Joy   112
   Walking Through Love's Dark Side   115
   Learning to Love   125
   The Sunshine of Our Attention   128
   Deeper Connections and Progress   134
   Making Meaning and Living the Good-Enough Life   140

Home   149

Bibliography   152

Acknowledgements   164

Index   165

Getting Started

> Never give up... No one knows what's going to happen next.
> - L. Frank Baum, *The Wonderful Wizard of Oz*

The classic children's book *The Wonderful Wizard of Oz*, by Frank Baum, showed generations of young readers how to remain true to their heart as they set out on life's path. Along the way, the characters encountered the glittering promise of magic and the frightening realities of loss. They learned to understand their fears and strengths, and by the end of the journey, they recognized the powers they had all along.

Like Oz, the world of autism seems to offer a simultaneous mix of magic, mystery, and horror. This book offers a way to help parents of autistic children see through that mix. We hope to show you, as the good witch showed Dorothy, that you have the power to learn, that there is science and a community of many people to help you on your way, and that it is possible to be happy to go home.

At this moment, home may seem like a hard place. Parenting and family life may have slipped far from how you imagined it would be. You might be afraid. Perhaps you are not in crisis but you're wondering whether you need to do some things, or many things, differently because someone you love has autism. For your family, the challenge is straightforward: daily life with autism. There is a way forward. Many families learn how to make progress. Many families find new dreams. They are happy. Their children are happy.

You may feel alone, but you are not. As a society, we are learning to understand the needs of the growing number of people diagnosed with autism. Yet, the advances bring a paradox of clarity and confusion. For many years, professionals worked to understand children who were different in how they communicated and interacted with other people, as well as the interests and activities they pursued. The autism label emerged to describe these children. As an umbrella, the label covers a wide range of ways of being. As a concept, autism remains an idea being built. In the best cases, the label helps people access opportunities and well-being. In the worst cases, the label is limiting and restrictive. Both professionals and autistic people are constantly reconstructing the meaning and boundaries of autism. Through this book and the work to come, you and your child will begin to learn and reconstruct the meanings and boundaries in your own ways.

When the autism label first emerged a few generations ago, this new social construct also came with a sentence: parents are inadequate and individuals must be institutionalized. There was no treatment. Doctors told parents to take their autistic child to a state institution and never look back. This posed an agonizing conflict. Life at home could offer no hope, but no parent wanted their child to live in an institution. Little knowledge, resources, or people were available to support families. During those times, policymakers didn't allocate time and resources to people with disabilities. Scientists were just beginning to understand how learning works. They were also discovering the magnitude of change that can happen when parents and professionals create an environment that allows dignity and growth. Moreover, communities didn't understand their collective responsibility to people with disabilities. This was a time of injustice and disgrace.

The times have changed. Reforms followed as society advanced its views about children's rights, worth, and capacities. This societal shift included children with autism and other disabilities. Early autism research showed promise, and our understanding deepened over the past fifty years. Researchers learned how to change the conditions that limited options for autistic children. Science and society stopped blaming parents, and many children saw their possibilities expand. Yet, while treatment services became more widely available, that growing availability hasn't guaranteed consistent or equitable progress on the journey. Autism services have entered the health care system. Autism is a profitable industry.

As treatment centers serve ever more clients, the relationships among practitioners, children, and families become fragile. Some families have begun to accept services without question, even as interventions are mass-produced and the needed collaboration around their child shrinks. Early in the development of effective interventions, parents were on the front line as partners in creating programs. They often educated themselves as advocates, too. Now, as interventions scale up, the institutional frameworks often discourage parents from learning the foundations of intervention or creating conditions that fit their child's unique needs and suit their family. The sense of urgency that once mobilized parents is gone.

Instead, the needed collaboration between parents and professionals fades as mass-produced treatment programs increase.

Professionals are pushing back against these developments. They recognize that the treatment arrangements often do not allot enough time for them to develop genuine relationships and partnerships with families. The recommended protocols have become increasingly rigid, crowding out conditions that foster professionals' responsiveness to the human being in front of them. Many treatment centers are located in medical complexes, strip malls, or shopping centers, far from places where other children are learning, playing, and building friendships. Parents sign in at the center, hand their child over to the health care provider, and return at the end of the session or the end of the day. Many direct providers who spend hours with the children all day long have never met the parents. In other words, children and therapists are being segregated from families and communities, likely at great physical, emotional, and spiritual costs.

Autistic adults are pushing back against these developments, too. Some say the treatment they received ostensibly as children in need of a cure produced harm. Others say the early intervention was indispensable and changed the possibilities that they encountered in life. This leads us to believe that different people are having very different experiences under the umbrella of "treatment."

Autism may have physical and biological attributes, but the way we respond to individuals with autism lies within a social construct. How we respond can hinder the possibilities—no different from the effects of buildings without ramps, movies without captions, or busy intersections without audio cues. Our society has built-in vulnerabilities that trigger frustration and anger for individuals with all types of disabilities. In addition, autistic adults remind us that autism brings its own gifts and strengths. Looking ahead, we can expect the autistic community to shape its own future, similar to the deaf community's movement for broad acceptance of sign language and deaf culture. From advocacy for the autistic label to the value of the emerging culture, the autistic community will be heard and relationships will be renegotiated.

In other words, autism is not the enemy. Some families, particularly families with young children new to the diagnosis, may be confused by this statement and feel even more isolated in meeting their responsibilities to their children. The most important thing to remember is that the essence of parenting—and living—involves learning, connecting, and loving. Accordingly, this book is meant to help parents practice these three powers. We hope that these pages release the heart's potential of every parent as they raise their autistic child and send them into the world. We ask, respectfully, for professionals to bear witness to the strength and joy that families are capable of summoning and to learn about the processes of strengthening family power.

Our Message: Learning, Connecting, and Loving with Intention

True courage is in facing danger when you are afraid …
- L. Frank Baum, *The Wonderful Wizard of Oz*

ودع

We have a responsibility to raise our children with autism as best we can. Parents cannot sidestep this journey. This work is part of how we all develop as humans—nurturing children in ways that honor their humanity and invite full, rich lives. Although access is not universal, we now have policies and laws that provide access to interventions and services so that children with autism can remain at home and learn and thrive in their communities. We have a budding science that demonstrates the power and promise of behavior change. And we have each other. Together, we are preparing pathways that offer hope and agency for people diagnosed with autism.

We offer this book as a roadmap for a joyful and sustainable journey. The essence of this journey relies on learning, connecting, and loving. Each power informs the other. Each amplifies the other. And each power is essential for meaningful and courageous parenting.

Science has begun the labor of illuminating how learning works. In **Part One: The Power of Learning**, we describe the science of behavior, which include the principles of learning and how they translate to action, as well as the methods and data behind an effective action. The ethics and care that professionals bring to teaching are also important to learning, including how parents can imbue love and wisdom in the entire process.

Learning is fundamental to raising any child but takes on special meaning for every single person involved in an autistic child's life. There is still much that researchers and practitioners do not know, but we do know that the specifics of learning are different for individuals with autism than for individuals without autism.

The understanding still needed in research, practice, parenting, and human and social development makes learning a key value and practice for everyone involved. We illustrate crucial concepts about learning with stories from unexpected places: read on to learn how piloting an airplane, repairing a clothes dryer, or baking a pound cake can inform the autism journey. We also show that families can channel this new knowledge to seek happier connections, in actions such as coming together as a family to enjoy a meal.

The learning process may seem akin to tackling a "how-to" list, which can be both a practical and problematic way to think about it. Problems can emerge when the work proceeds in an unresponsive, rigid, check-the-box manner. Problems can also emerge when we are only looking for ways to escape a hard situation, rather than build a dream. To bring responsive wisdom instead, parents can seek to build a constructive community around them and their child.

In **Part Two: The Power of Connecting**, we describe the energy and wisdom the people around us bring as we nurture our child and our family. In addition to working with friends and family, parents can collaborate with professionals, who can be powerful partners on the journey. Connecting to one another fosters shared growth. Connecting also strengthens the compass that maintains quality in a child's care as well as a keen responsiveness to their needs. In this section, we share stories of families surrounded by and connected to others who respect and reflect their values and give more energy and ideas for progress. Often, that progress outshines what a parent could have done alone. This work may seem magical at times, but we offer a closer look to reveal that generous connections often share the same qualities, such as reciprocity, resilience, and learning from one another.

Connecting to others helps families find wisdom and meaning in what may otherwise seem like chaos. This meaning-making is vital to learning and loving. At the end of this section, we suggest ways and places to find connections in the community. Our community belonging can boost relationships, well-being, and happiness.

Love is at the core of what we choose to do with our children and why we choose it. Care and kindness can guide how we do the work. Dreams influence the choices we make, and our actions can have implications twenty years down the road. In **Part Three: The Power of Loving**, we describe love's boundless capacity to foster learning and bring deeper meaning to our connections with others. Love is the joyful, animating force behind both the family and the professional. Yet, some families don't start out with the same access to resources that others have. These varying conditions have become more transparent as marginalized communities speak out. In this section, we show how the power of loving (as well as learning and connecting) applies under all conditions. We include stories of families whose wise, loving actions met their responsibilities and expanded the possibilities for justice. We also examine love's dark side, those situations of fear, anger, and desperation that we rarely talk about. Through an understanding of the emotional dark corners, we show how families have created spaces of light and found direction and purpose.

By focusing on these three powers, this book shows how to envision the most constructive, least restrictive pathways toward a fulfilling and joyful life in which our children can make their own decisions as they grow.

Shahla's Message

It is a wonderful and awkward thing for two writers to tell a story together. There are no easy formulas for collective telling. With each exploration and each story in this book, we talked until we found shared truths. We then had to describe them so that readers could see what we were seeing.

What we share in these pages may sometimes be easy to see, especially for readers who are already on that part of the journey and have some sense of the importance of the three powers in that situation. For example, a reader searching for an early intervention provider may already be learning what to look for, who to ask, and how to trust their instincts that a provider will or won't protect and nourish their child. We know that at other times, the terrain we explore will likely feel as unfamiliar as Mars—for example, what happens to our child when we die?

Late in the summer of 1995, I sat in Peggy's little house by the railroad tracks with my firstborn in my arms. We were watching her three kids play in creative, happy ways, and I was getting breastfeeding advice. Peggy was generous and practical. I was anxious and fretting. One thing you have to know about Peggy is that she is brave. I always imagine that if I had known her when we were both eight years old, I would have been watching her teach herself to gracefully dive off the highest board. Meanwhile, I would have been trying to figure out how she negotiated the line of ladder bullies, while simultaneously thinking, "Ha! Maybe I can do that, too."

About ten years later, both of our worlds started to shift. We had covered a lot of ground together working with police education programs, toy-lending libraries, and autism special interest groups. Peggy had written a book, I'd gotten tenure, and our children were well. Then, my mother was diagnosed with dementia and my father with late-stage lung cancer. The worst was yet to come. Mark, Peggy's husband, was killed in a tragic accident. These were hard years.

After the fallout from these events, we took a short road trip together. Texas Parent-to-Parent, a nonprofit that provides services to parents and caregivers of children with disabilities, held its annual conference in San Marcos, where we gave a joint talk about guides that can help caregivers make decisions. Afterward, late into the night, we started talking about loss and feeling lost. We both found wisdom and strength from shared belief systems about life after death. Many spiritual traditions teach that all souls continue after death and that those souls accompany us on our earthly journey, guiding us in finding our meaning on this earth.

This book offers you our guiding stories. We frame the meaning of the stories and emphasize their messages, but what lies ahead is the intentional journey of your own life as well as the process of learning and making meaning. There is no escaping your own labor. It is a labor that goes beyond your child. It is about you and how you walk in life. Over time, we have come to understand that as parents, we are responsible for these beautiful souls we helped bring into the world. And, like them, we each have our own journey. The intertwined nature of this relationship is a balance. It is about us and our children and also about the separateness of each of us in becoming. From our perspective on the parenting and professional journeys, and from our grandmother-like vantage points, we hope to accompany you in developing your power and meaning.

Peggy's Message

A line from the movie *You've Got Mail* almost steals the show when the main characters first meet across the counter in a children's book store. "When you read a book as a child, it becomes a part of your identity in a way that no other reading in your whole life does," one character says to the other. Credit for this bit of wisdom likely belongs to screenwriter Nora Ephron. Gifted writers wend their way into our hearts and stay in our thoughts long after we turn the last page of their book. Even as an adult, each time I open a book, I hope to see and feel the world in a new way, just as I did as a girl.

When my son Sam was diagnosed with autism, I read many books. It took a long time to cobble together the ideas and perspective to help me see and feel the world as Sam needed me to do, and to understand what was happening and how to move in new directions. The University of North Texas Press published my first book about that struggle, *See Sam Run*.

I was also lucky to have met Shahla early on. Both of us had come from families with limited resources and entered the workforce as teens. Our families believed in the power of education and were committed to social change. She supplied knowledge to fill gaps in some of the books I'd been reading. She often served as a touchstone as Sam headed in bold, new directions. Sometimes I would forget the nature of her work and her field because I saw her as my sister, confidant, and friend. But now and then, I'd glimpse an idea or perspective that we'd discussed and how it was shaping her work and her world. Then, I would remember what a smart, sensitive clinician and scientist she is. Shahla listens and responds.

This book evolved after Shahla and I started talking about the core values of her work—things like acceptance, humility, generosity, and compassion—and how they could be best communicated to the people around us. The ideas went through many iterations, workshops, and drafts. We didn't set out to model connecting and collaborating when we started the book, but we quickly recognized that the best way this book could become a part of your identity was to make it a part of ours. Welcome.

A Note on the Tools, Methodology, and Terms We Use

Drop by drop is the water pot filled. Likewise, the wise man, gathering it little by little, fills himself with good.
- The Buddha

This book reflects our own cumulative learning and is organized in a way that tells how we, too, developed ourselves through learning, connecting, and loving. We thought for a long time about the durability of these three powers, particularly since we gave the talk on decision-making at the Parent-to-Parent conference.

The word "power" is both a noun and a verb, articulating the capacity and the energy to do important things. As a capacity to raise an emerging human, parenting powers can be learned. As an energy, parenting powers can also be a great force in a family's life. We can all learn new things, develop relationships, and nourish love. Together, these powers can and will direct the course of a child's development in meaningful ways. Stories of how others developed and used their powers provide good examples for learning. We deliberately include a range of examples to illustrate the central concepts of each power.

We occasionally offer specific, practical advice on how to develop these capacities for your child's benefit. Yet, this book does not contain checklists. Checklists are terrific for basic tasks like going to the grocery store. The checklist works because the environment and the shopper's needs tend to remain constant. The list serves as a memory aid for buying bread, milk, paper products, and frozen things. Shoppers also feel less stress going up and down the grocery aisles, confident in the checklist for tracking what they need and avoiding the hassle of returning home, having forgotten something important.

Checklists can also help with important, routine tasks—from editing a newspaper, to getting a mammogram, to preparing a surgeon's tools. Such checklists help workers follow a proven sequence that avoids costly errors and aids their focus on higher-level thinking. For example, when a mammogram technician adheres to the required sequence, neither the patient nor the technician is exposed to excess radiation, and the resulting images accurately reflect what's happening in the body. In addition, the checklist allows the technician to focus on remaining caring and kind toward the patient, which can be especially reassuring at a stressful time.

Checklists offer less problem-solving power to complex, high-stakes issues, such as a complicated heart surgery or marriage counseling. Certainly, there are general guidelines for people involved in such stressful work, but surgeons and counselors help tackle these problems with power that goes beyond the steps outlined in a checklist.

You and your child are living and growing in a specific context that will need both checklists and deeper knowledge to help you make progress. You will face complex issues that can't always be solved with quick fixes or a prescribed series of tasks. All children grow up under a wide range of conditions, meaning, and emotions. In highly charged situations, checklists can sometimes be unproductive, especially when following the checklist becomes more important than noticing the person or challenge in front of us.

These more complex situations ask us to be responsive in ways guided by solid principles, methods, and values. Such problem-solving requires both the scientific method and our humanity. Therefore, throughout these pages, we offer guidance to help you explore three fundamental questions: What do you need to know? Who will help you? How can love be your constant compass?

We occasionally provide historical context since both behavior analysis and autism as a diagnosis are new events in human evolution. Shahla's career as an applied behavior analyst began as many researchers were discovering what they could do to help people with autism. She graduated from the University of Kansas at a dynamic time. Behavior analysis grew out of experimental psychology. Over time, behavior analysts developed worthwhile ways to help people make progress, without using techniques that most of us call punishment. They were also talking about their scientific discipline in new ways, including the importance of heart and collaboration in the process of changing behavior. They focused on a science built on compassion and continual progress (Part One further describes the development of autism research).

We also echo and add to ongoing discussions that are keeping the science of behavior analysis progressive today. Research and practice are in a state of flux, as they should be. Shahla works with children with autism in clinical practice, focusing on family progress and well-being. She also supports graduate students in gaining knowledge and compassionate clinical skills. By showing the power in how we help each other, how we talk and respond to each other, how we learn and bring meaning to our interactions, we can challenge the scaffolds that insurance companies, venture capitalists, and some education institutions have built around autism. By saying that love *and* progress matter, we can also challenge the pockets of mediocrity and the lack of heart and feeling in some services provided to children and their families. Happily, learning and connecting deliver the remedy to this mediocrity.

To illustrate many important ideas, we include stories from families and people with autism who have touched Shahla's life and from Peggy's and Sam's experiences. We relate Peggy's and Sam's experiences as they occurred. To honor the privacy of the children and families in Shahla's stories, we chose pseudonyms and created composite stories to protect privacy and retain confidentiality. Other examples come from books and research papers, and we retain the pseudonyms used in those publications. The appendix lists those references along with other recommended reading and resources.

For hypothetical examples, we use the pronouns "he," "she," and "they" interchangeably across (but not within) examples. We also use "autistic" and "child with autism" interchangeably. In those stories that are not composite cases and identify specific individuals, we have asked for and used that person's preferences for pronouns, names, and identities. Throughout the text, we often refer to children with autism as "our child" and to parents and professionals together as "we." We chose these references to reflect our perspectives as parents and practitioner. We believe that love, learning, and connection are key values and practices and that these word choices reflect a shared humanity, interdependence, and responsibility.

The three powers have served us well and are still serving us. How we learned to describe these powers for this book has taught us even more about them and reinforces our conviction that learning in a trusted, loving community brings bounty and is vital in the midst of both personal and global changes. Our families have benefited from this learning and from using these powers. We hope yours will, too.

Part One: The Power of Learning

> The scientific observer of Nature is a kind of mystic
> seeker in the act of prayer.
> - Muhammad Iqbal

Learning takes on special meaning for every person involved in an autistic child's life—from understanding the current science of how we all learn to tapping long-held wisdom about good parenting and improving the human condition.

We didn't have generations of medical practice or cultural wisdom to guide us when autism was first identified in the 1940s. Doctors, therapists, teachers, and parents had little information back when autism was considered rare. Many parents and professionals just gave up. Today, the diagnosis is more common. We know that children with autism can learn. Researchers initially did not understand how much motivation matters in the ways that people can learn, until they used scientific principles to approach, observe, and analyze human behavior. Motivation changes human behavior. For example, most children master the sound of the letter "r" quite late as they learn to talk, as late as five or six years old. But an autistic child who loves rockets might just master the "r" sound before mastering other sounds in human speech. In fact, rockets might have such profound importance to her that the topic and a good teacher can propel her motivation to learn other hard things, especially when a caring team honors those interests.

The science of behavior analysis and applied behavior analysis have deepened the understanding of how learning works. How, then, do we learn about this science? How do we find the right information for our needs? How do we sift through it all and make good decisions? After we hear about a promising finding, how can we be sure that we do good—and not harm—in putting that information to work for our child and our family? We can begin by gaining a basic understanding of the science of behavior and its principles.

In this section, we describe concepts for working with children to help them learn, how these ideas came about, and how they work. We also describe how this work can fail and how to address that. Knowing how behavior works, we can collaborate with professionals to use the science to help our child learn, encourage our family to stay connected, and increase the chances that our child will grow into a happy, productive, and healthy adult.

Yet, there is much that researchers and practitioners still do not know. Our ignorant responses in the face of the unknown are often stigmatizing. We therefore also describe some signs of ignorance and show how to shift toward seeking knowledge—our best chance to build loving practices and wisdom.

At the end of this section, we show how learning helps us observe patterns in our life and how we can imagine—even dream of—new possibilities. Learning to sit down as a family to enjoy a meal together, for example, builds knowledge that honors our child's humanity, our own cultures, and our family's connections.

In the Beginning

...with your courage and with your compassion and your desire, we will build a Great Society. It is a society where no child will go unfed, and no youngster will go unschooled.
- Lyndon B. Johnson

During the 1960s, President Lyndon B. Johnson declared a war on poverty, racism, and ignorance. The subsequent initiatives were concentrated in education and public human service reforms. Experimental psychologists, among other groups, responded to society's call for change. These psychologists had curious natures, big hearts, and believed in change. Their good work set a new path for understanding human development and changed the world we live in, particularly for people with autism and their families.

The zeitgeist of this call for a Great Society reflected both hope and action to make the world a better place. The early experimental psychologists (later called operant psychologists, behavior scientists, and applied behavior analysts) were among the Great Society's trailblazers. They ventured into institutions where no one else cared to go. They believed that change was possible for the people whom the rest of society had abandoned and forgotten. Using scientific methods, they discovered and demonstrated meaningful change. The science of applied behavior analysis advanced from that set of ideals.

We may already understand that science fosters some of the highest forms of learning about ourselves and the world around us. To understand applied behavior analysis, it is helpful to start by acknowledging the general nature and limitations of science. Scientific knowledge and findings bring new possibilities and meaning to our lives, but that knowledge also has parameters.

Scientists build knowledge in a progressive, intentional way. They direct their search with purpose and a deep regard for collective understanding among other scientists. In any discipline, scientific understanding is in a constant state of reflection and change. After splitting the atom, for example, physicists are diving ever deeper into the nature of matter.

Scientists use formal systems of study in their search for knowledge. This formality allows them to work collectively, using methods and rules to detect patterns in nature. Their methods and rules also guide their thinking about those patterns, what the patterns might mean, and how the patterns relate to one another. This formality, for example, allowed physician David Ho, an HIV researcher, and mathematician Alan Perelson to team up to solve a pernicious problem: the virus's drug resistance. They discovered that a three-drug cocktail helps patients live long lives and avoid AIDS, the late stage of HIV infection.

The more that any science moves into real life, that is, the more it is applied, the more it can improve the well-being of people and society. The basic research into the nature of the HIV virus, for example, jump-started the applied research that allowed the quick development of effective COVID-19 vaccines.

In human behavior, applied behavior scientists develop methods to understand how people behave when changes occur in physical or social environments. They also study the issues that matter to humanity right now. In this work, they are obliged to build knowledge and improve conditions for the people who need the benefits of that research in the first place. In other words, ethics and science are in a constant, intertwined dance.

Science is both wonderful and frustrating. Scientists learn great things, but the knowledge always comes with more uncertainty. In addition, the methods used to gain that knowledge have sometimes produced pain and trauma. For example, evolutionary biology produced some of the knowledge to develop COVID-19 vaccines, but the work also produced eugenics (which promotes selective breeding of human populations to improve genetic composition). Modern obstetrics allows for the healthy delivery of twins, but many practices were learned through experimenting on the reproductive organs of Black enslaved women who received no anesthesia.

Discoveries about the autistic brain reflect basic research with a dark history, too. In recent decades, several families have selflessly donated brain tissue after losing their autistic loved one. The information helped reveal patterns that led to scientific discoveries after researchers compared the tissue to a world data bank—a data bank of brain tissue first built by doctors of the Third Reich.

Similar tensions have emerged in autism intervention. These tensions revolve around identifying what behaviors should be changed and why, and under what conditions. Both science and society are negotiating and understanding how to proceed so that the work retains dignity, fosters well-being, and balances the needs of individuals and communities.

These realities remind us that scientific discovery is both a social and political act, and each scientist's pursuit comes in its own social context. Why does this matter? To live and thrive in our sophisticated world, we benefit from understanding science and how it progresses and that includes the science around our child with autism. As we learn new things about the world of autism and begin to make decisions for our child, we will find much evidence, promise, discussion, debate, anger, and trauma. It's confusing, so we may be easily lured away by the person or group that says they have the answer.

In the midst of this we can remember that good professionals rely on families to learn, too. Clinicians can apply the scientific method to their practice, following both systematic rules and ethical responsibilities. Parents have information that can guide this applied science, to ensure that their child is on a path to become the architect and agent of their own life to the greatest degree possible and balance their rights and responsibilities as they grow up in the community.

Looking at the early studies in autism can elicit both smiles and shudders. The first study that showed true possibilities involved a young autistic boy named Dicky. The life that Dicky and his family experienced before treatment was harsh: severe distress, a lot of medication, probably very little joy, and Dicky's possible removal from home. Taking one set of goals at a time, operant psychologists Montrose Wolf, Todd Risley, and Hayden Mees at the University of Washington worked with Dicky in the early 1960s. First, they collaborated with his family and considered what was likely to improve his life as well as what was making his life difficult. Dicky was not reduced to a label or diagnosis to be treated. He was a child with things to learn and things to change. Their work was scientific: they conceptualized, controlled, and documented the work they did and the progress they made. During the intervention, Dicky initially spent a lot of time in seclusion as a consequence for some of his behavior (shudder). He was also gently guided, step by step, to wear glasses that prevented him from going blind (smiles). Even in the context of a new and somewhat crude science, a kind of miracle occurred in Dicky's life. Dicky and his family found joy. Together with family and professionals, this young boy forged an independent, happy life, free from the harsh ways of institutional confinement. At the time, people had thought such an outcome was impossible.

Since that time, researchers have discovered ways to reduce both distress and the use of seclusion as well as to increase the time spent in quality teaching. Science progressed. In its collective and intentional way, science has helped us learn that a child's tantrum is a form of communication. Dicky had tantrums. The professionals and parents worked with Dicky step by step to help him communicate, thereby reducing the conditions that left Dicky hurting himself. Applied behavior scientists have since built a body of knowledge that develops ways to communicate, rather than relying on punishment to reduce problem behaviors. We've come a long way.

Yet, science remains political. Some behavior analysts have been paid to stop autistic children's behaviors that bother people. Because these practitioners were kind souls, they spent significant time figuring out how to do that in a loving way. But our society does not place much emphasis on building new behaviors until there is a problem. We often wait and respond to a problem, rather than working toward a dream. That means that systematic knowledge of how we shape complex language and make friends has not developed as rapidly as how we reduce problem behavior, even though this is part of what early researchers were learning. That's on us, as a society. We need to be part of the evolution of what science studies and learns to change.

Still, the pioneering work with Dicky set the precedent for a particular way of having hope and making progress. After the 1964 publication documenting Dicky's progress, a flurry of determined activity followed in the late 1960s and the 1970s. Behavior scientists replicated and extended the first experiments with more experiments. They developed additional, more powerful ways to change behavior for the better. Researchers determined which behaviors to target and how and when to change them to affect the course of a child's development. Starting with Dicky in 1964 and culminating in 1973 with key findings by O. Ivar Lovaas, Robert Koegel, James Q. Simmons, and Judith Steven Long, scientists demonstrated that children with autism and other disabilities could learn.

Until the early 1970s, children with autism and other disabilities were often institutionalized. Television journalist Geraldo Rivera broadcast a jarring exposé nationwide in 1972, calling these institutions "the last great disgrace" of human civilization. A year later, in 1973, Lovaas and his colleagues demonstrated the power to change behavior for the better in many children. In one of the sadder notes from this period, they also showed that the progress disintegrated when the children returned to institutional life. Most of the children lost nearly everything they had gained.

Then came Lovaas's breakthrough study published in 1987. Lovaas and his students revised the protocols and procedures from the earlier studies. They worked with younger autistic children, and they worked with intensity and vigor. They involved the children's parents. They worked for hours every day, wherever the children were, whatever they were doing, and whomever they were with. In other words, they made the behavioral intervention as pervasive as the difficulties.

In 1996, Catherine Maurice's book *Let Me Hear Your Voice* increased popular understanding of this new kind of intervention. She explained the research by describing, with detail and nuance, the work with her two children diagnosed with autism. Maurice sought information and allies when her children were preschoolers. Therapists came to their home for many hours each day to work with them on hundreds of skills, including learning to imitate, to speak, and to use the toilet. The therapists responded to the children with warmth and enthusiasm as they systematically planned small steps of rapid progress. They also worked with the family.

When her book debuted, readers were astonished by the outcomes possible for children with autism. Maurice acknowledged Lovaas's pivotal role in charting the possibilities, even as she had reservations about some of the methods. Because she had written her story in a way that allowed people to better understand the science and practice of applied behavior analysis, the book created a broad demand for autism services, a demand that has continued. That demand, in turn, created a marketplace.

Science for Sale

Science knows no country, because knowledge belongs to humanity, and is the torch which illuminates the world.
- Louis Pasteur

When the experimental psychologists answered society's call for change, they didn't set out to create a new marketplace. They wanted to learn about the world in a new way. They wanted to alleviate suffering. They wanted to improve quality of life. However, as others learned and expanded their discoveries, and after families advocated for more support and services, more people with autism received help. On one hand, today children are learning, some at accelerated and astonishing speed. Few autistic children must live in institutions. On the other hand, some children aren't learning, and some children are traumatized. All of this new scientific knowledge and its application have big implications for parents and professionals.

Autism services have entered the health care system and have become a profitable industry. The interventions bring wonderful, lasting progress when delivered with intention, skill, effort, and love. Interventions that lack those qualities can be arbitrary and fruitless. As some providers have scaled up their business to serve increasing numbers of children, the relationship between providers and families has become fragile and the treatment protocols less individualized. In other words, growth hasn't guaranteed progress. When interventions became an object of trade, that change triggered new questions and concerns. We cannot ignore that treatment has become a billion-dollar industry in which each part of a child can be both a therapeutic opportunity and a capital venture. Pieces of autism have become big business.

Mickey Keenan and his colleagues outlined some of these concerns in their 2010 article "Science for Sale: But at What Price?" They asked important questions about the unscrupulous promotion of scientific findings in autism. Do the findings translate into commodities that only some children and families can access? Is it ethical to provide fewer or degraded services when there isn't enough money or there is lack of understanding about the cultural context? The questions don't stop there. We extend Keenan's list: What happens when parts of a child's disability are considered financial opportunities and treatment is provided with profit as the priority? What happens when some children's bodies are valued more than others because of their race, gender, ethnicity, or income? Will commodification influence the direction that behavior science researchers take? Has it already?

Researchers and clinicians have ethical guidelines to address at least some of these questions, implications, and complications. Behavior analysts are required to include parents, family members, other caregivers, and the child in the decision-making for any interventions or treatment plans. Clinicians should ask their peers to review a proposed intervention for the potential to do harm and the potential to provide benefit. They need to know when it's unethical to intervene in a behavior and when it's okay to target a behavior for change. And if the planned intervention involves children and their families in a research project, clinicians and researchers must follow additional protective guidelines required by law and implemented by the research institution. Those guidelines minimize the potential for harm, while increasing the potential for benefit and each child's well-being.

Similarly, behavior science research and autism interventions in clinical practice affect each other in complicated ways, which raises the stakes for treatment when delivered by an industry driven by profit motives. Behavioral research and interventions work differently from the ways we treat other health problems. Medical doctors see an illness as pathological. They prescribe drugs or order surgery to help us get better. Sometimes we experience side effects. But for the most part, submitting to medical treatment doesn't require much effort on our part. We might suffer, but we often get better without continuous effort.

Behavioral interventions don't work that way. To change human behavior, we decide where we want to be and we build a path to get there.

New behavior builds on other behavior. We teach our child with autism to talk, to share, and to play with blocks. Then, once our child can talk, share, and play, he has a foundation to learn more. In other words, the behavioral interventions are constructional, not pathological. Behavioral treatment requires time, skill, and effort from everyone doing the building: the parents, the professionals, and the child. It is not easy.

It's human nature to avoid work that requires effort or doesn't produce immediate results. But if we grab at the promise of a quick cure or seek to make progress with little effort, we make ourselves vulnerable to complex dangers. The bottom line for autism families is this: we should be skeptical of therapies that seem too easy, don't need constant calibration, or don't require our collaboration. Even more suspect are therapies that lack scientific support, particularly when people delivering the treatment are making a profit.

We can also think about behavior science's constructive approach in another way: we can stop seeing our autistic child as diseased. Instead, we can pivot toward learning and making specific progress for her needs. We can remain open to opportunity so her life can expand as much as possible. We work with her so she can learn skills. We may also need to work with the community (school, day care, church, mosque, synagogue, government, business) to better accommodate her and other individuals with autism.

In addition, to better understand this constructive approach, we can keep in mind a key principle of learning and science. Progress is inherent in science, including behavior science. Sometimes, the interplay between behavior science research and autism treatment can appear one-directional. That is, we might think that the all-knowing scientist first gives a formula, and then the clinician and family follow the treatment prescription. But the knowledge developed in behavior science and autism treatment flows both to and from researchers and clinicians, or at least it should.

Moreover, any science is a process of discovery. In the best circumstances, research and clinical practice respect and inform each other. Clinicians and researchers test and retest, refine, and redefine their interventions. With discoveries come new questions, and some questions will be unexpected. New discoveries can bring previous research into sharper focus. Sometimes new discoveries reinforce ancient wisdom. New discoveries can also shift the paradigm, upending old understandings and suggesting new paths for deeper scientific knowledge.

This means that our child's treatment comes with gray areas of scientific understanding. We can be ready for the possibility that the scientific support for an idea, treatment, or behavioral intervention may change.

We can also resist the temptation to be like the Monday morning quarterback who second-guesses the big plays, deciding, for example, that a time out or a slap on the bottom is all that's needed for our child's progress. When we take shortcuts, we introduce unnecessary risk into our child's life. Instead, we can study the basic playbook to learn more and seek a team with skilled players and coaches.

A Science of Love and Change

Research is to see what everybody else has seen and think what nobody has thought.
- Arthur Schopenhauer

When parents know a little about the basics of behavior analysis and its technology, they can participate in their child's learning at a deeper level. Parents don't have to be scientists to grasp the building blocks of behavior science and its technology. Any science is a specific discipline that focuses on a process and how it works, as well as the methods to improve that process for many different situations. The applied science of behavior analysis focuses on behavior, how it works, and which methods improve behavior in different situations and in ways that the participants and society value. Technology applies the scientific knowledge for practical purposes. For example, computers are a technology for math and modeling. We can build a technology for our child's learning by participating in it. The work may not be part of the larger body of behavior science and its technology, but we are building a technology that is specific to our child's well-being. To build that technology, we begin by learning the basics of how behavior change works.

Human behavior is anything we do: walking and dancing, talking and laughing, reading and arguing. Behavior science has vocabulary for things that happen both before (antecedent stimuli) and after (reinforcing or punishing consequences) a behavior. Behavior scientists also consider what a behavior looks like (structure) and the behavior's effect on the environment (function). To better understand what affects behavior, researchers look for order and patterns. They also look at the social and physical environments around behaviors. What comes before and after a behavior is important, as is the timing of the things that come before and after. The dependent relations between those events are called contingencies. The before, during, and after of behavior and the environment have little meaning without the analysis of their relationships to one another.

The applied behavior analyst uses knowledge of the timing and relationships to develop contingencies that will shape new skills. In this way, we create responses and conditions that foster growth and change in our child and affect outcomes for the long term. If we view a behavior as relationships among a sequence of parts, then we can shift our response in more powerful ways. In this analysis of before, during, and after, one of the most important things behavior scientists have learned is the power of preferred things following a behavior. These preferred things are timed as consequences. They reinforce the behavior; they increase the chances that whatever they follow will happen again. The systematic use of reinforcers is one of the ways that Dicky learned to use his glasses and that Catherine Maurice's children learned to talk.

But there is more. Reinforcers both sustain a behavior and, if managed well, can provide further opportunity. We can position reinforcers in ways that help a child make progress in many areas: walking and talking, playing ball and riding a tricycle, eating and reading, doing chores and taking care of a sibling, dancing and laughing. Our child will be attracted to particular events under different conditions and contexts. This is a law in human behavior in the same way that gravity's attracting force is a law in physics. Moreover, we all—ourselves, family members, friends, teachers, therapists, researchers, and even insurance companies and payment providers—have both individual and shared attractions.

Some of the best reinforcers include everyone, such as toys that encourage and sustain our child's social interactions with us and others. The social interactions themselves can be reinforcers, even if a little odd at first. The more the reinforcers serve as a common denominator for everyone, the more the reinforcers can be expanded and redirected to connect our child to others and learning. When our child shares reinforcers with the rest of the world, she is less likely to be left out.

Let's consider different possible reinforcers for a child who is being loud and disrupting class by drumming on their desk. One child may drum, and the teacher's attention reinforces the action because, for this child, even a scolding can be a reinforcer. Another child may drum, and their action is reinforced because they escaped a difficult task—after all, it's hard to complete a task when one is busy drumming and being scolded. Yet another child may be so enamored by the sound of the drumming that they do not notice they are being scolded; in addition, finishing the assigned task isn't relevant to them.

Different children will find different reinforcers in the same set of circumstances. Furthermore, let's consider how that whole picture changes when the conditions change: a child is drumming outside and there are many children and adults on a playground with the drummer. The same people will have different reinforcers under different conditions. The child's drumming might go unnoticed on the playground; for some children, swings are more interesting than drumming; other children might join in the drumming; drumming and singing could be the primary activity of the older, esteemed kids; the echoes of drumming on the playground equipment might be reinforcing; and so on. In other words, reinforcement depends on many things. Therefore, we say that something is reinforcing by its effect on behavior.

All those different preferences and choices affect the environment and complicate our work in building a path to a new behavior. One area of behavior science devotes itself to studying only reinforcement: how to assess it, how it develops, how experience changes responses, how other reinforcers alter value.

Here's an example of how complicated that scientific process can be: a hungry lab animal will respond to conditions a certain way after learning that those responses bring food. Researchers who have been studying the animal's behavior for a while can change the conditions and stop delivering food to see what other behaviors might return. In this way, researchers gain a more sophisticated understanding of two behavioral principles related to reinforcement: extinction (behaviors that stop after they no longer produce the desired result) and resurgence (previously learned behaviors that return under certain conditions). Researchers and clinicians are still learning how these basic principles relate to human behavior. But some clinicians deploy what we know now about resurgence so that they can sustain caring, trusting relationships with their clients and their families.

For example, Shahla worked with a two-year-old boy, Noah, and his mother to learn how to lovingly communicate with one another during a teaching program. First, they worked to understand what Noah liked and disliked. Shahla and Noah's mother determined how best to regulate access to what he liked so that through the process of reinforcement, they could teach him as quickly as possible to select and communicate his own preferences. Every human needs effective, courteous ways to communicate their needs and preferences. Children can learn early on how to communicate graciously, and others can learn how to respond enthusiastically and positively to them in those communications.

The harder treatment gets—and it nearly always does—the farther back a child is likely to go in their learning history to respond. Behaviors make a comeback. We can make sure, by design, that when the work gets hard, whatever happens next reinforces the loving, trusting relationship between us and our child, as well as the therapists.

Noah liked collecting poker chips and Matchbox cars and playing with water. His mother and Shahla's team invented lots of different games to capitalize on these preferences that made him happy. His mother would offer poker chips that he could put in a coffee can, or she'd fill a tub of water in which he could float his plastic fish. Whenever he made a noise, put his hands up, or made eye contact with her, she responded by handing over the toys. She was reinforcing any positive social interactions that seemed directed toward her. By doing this, she established that any attempt he made to interact, short of running away screaming, was good and communicative.

Next, the therapists and Noah's mother worked with him to learn to imitate, a core skill that children with autism need. One of the ways children learn how to learn is by observing and imitating the world around them. Many children with autism don't learn this way. Noah needed to be able to imitate so that he could learn from watching others, learn how to talk, and learn how to play. To begin, Noah's mother made a game with toy fish and water, two things he loved. She would say "bloop, bloop" and wait for any sign of connection—a gaze or an arm outstretched, for example. Once she saw his intention and attempt, she'd hand over the fish, one at a time. When the fish splashed, Noah would quiver and smile.

After establishing that foundation of sustained gaze, Noah's mother moved to the harder skill of imitation. Noah got access to the fish after he made any sounds, and then, after he imitated her specific sounds. Sometimes the sounds she made were too hard to imitate, or she jumped ahead too far. She was learning, too. When Noah found it hard to imitate his mother and didn't get immediate access to the next toy fish, she saw his struggle and handed over the toy when he just looked at her or tugged her arm. Together, they created a foundation that reinforced their loving relationship as they both figured out how to learn together. A little at a time, she changed what she required of Noah so that it was doable and enjoyable. And he let her know when it wasn't working.

In this way, therapists can use both reinforcement, a central concept in the science of behavior, and resurgence, a concept from the basic branch of the science, to design teaching programs in an effective, practical, loving way. Noah's mother and Shahla intentionally laid a foundation for a comeback response that was connected and safe and would allow them to adjust the teaching sequence. It could have been different. If Noah had been forced, if his beloved fish had been withheld for too long, for too much or too little effort, or not given in a way that was appreciated, or taken away with cruelty, his comeback response could have been haunting—rage, resignation, or self-injury.

The skilled use of reinforcement is powerful. The success, failure, comfort, and discomfort resulting from reinforcement procedures rely on a repertoire of knowledge and skills, such as understanding the timing, the history of the timing, the assessment of preferences, and the responsiveness to the child's response in the moment and over time. It is a new science, but it has developed powerful knowledge in a short period. It can work in complicated environments and produce sophisticated skills.

For example, when Peggy's son Sam was in second grade, he had a hard time focusing in class. He got up from his chair often. He looked out the window. He checked the clock. His teacher wasn't able to work with Sam so that he could stay focused on some of the lessons. She called Peggy and told her that Sam's wandering attention could become a long-term problem. In second grade, children are still learning to read. But by third and fourth grade, they read to learn. As the pace of teaching and learning quickened, Sam could get behind, perhaps hopelessly so.

The teacher started sending Sam out into the hallway with the teacher's aide when he couldn't sit still or when he made noises that distracted the other children. Sam studied some lessons with the aide in the hallway.

After a few weeks, Sam was spending more time out in the hallway than in class.

One of the aides called Peggy because Sam was starting to miss other lessons. More important, Sam was not learning how to focus. Instead, the teacher was reinforcing Sam's wandering by sending him out to the hallway. The hallway was easier. Peggy asked for help from an education professor, Kevin Callahan, who designed a self-management program for Sam and the teachers. This program was based on the work of Robert and Lynn Koegel, longtime researchers in autism intervention. Kevin explained the basic behavioral principles of the intervention to the teacher and the aides. Then they worked with Sam to learn to monitor his own attention. Kevin made a tape that beeped at random intervals. At key times during class, Sam would hear a quiet beep at his desk, and he would know to ask himself three questions: Am I in my seat? Am I working quietly? Am I looking at my teacher or my materials?

Sam scored himself on each question. His aide also scored him. Sam knew he would earn more points if he scored himself accurately. He learned to assess himself. He cashed his points for items he liked: pencils, folders, small toys, and candy. Kevin and a graduate student collected and analyzed the data on the score sheets. They saw that Sam began to sit still more often than not. He worked quietly and appeared to be paying attention. The aides and the teacher agreed that Sam was on task more often than before the intervention began.

However, Sam's reading and math grades dropped. Kevin pressed the teacher and aides for information. If Sam was paying attention, shouldn't his grades reflect increased comprehension? The teacher and the aides told him they weren't surprised that Sam's grades had dipped because he was doing much more of his work by himself. His grades bounced back in time.

Peggy didn't know until much later that Sam's grades had suffered during that period. She was surprised to learn those details after they happened and discovered an important lesson about the big picture in such situations. When Kevin expressed his concerns about Sam's grades to the teacher and the aides, Peggy wasn't part of that conversation. Granted, final grade reports provide feedback for parents. However, because parents care about their children's long-term well-being, the parents' knowledge and perspective bring value to such discussions. Peggy may have been able to help with the short-term grade dip. Parents and caregivers should be part of assessments and decisions in a child's treatment plan. In fact, as much as a researcher, teacher, or interventionist is trained to understand complex and sophisticated procedures, they only gain their importance and usefulness in the context of the child making progress. Parents are key to that happening. Their participation in such discussions and decision-making also helps them learn more about their child.

Such teaching programs might seem simple and doable. Sometimes they are; sometimes they aren't. The behavioral processes involved in Noah's and Sam's experiences, for example, are actually quite involved. In Noah's case, researchers and clinicians have learned a great deal about how the timing of reinforcement works to shape conventional speech, and they are just starting to learn about how the process can be designed to affect a more positive relationship (in technical terms, the synchronicity of reinforcement between the parent and child).

Similarly, in Sam's case, researchers know the strategy works, but details of its effectiveness remain unclear. Specifically, researchers are just beginning to understand the way that cues (in technical terms, stimulus control) and preferred activities (in technical terms, potential reinforcers) combine to help a person become a reliable observer of their own behavior. Researchers and clinicians are still learning and debating the chain of events—an individual observing their own behavior, following the rule, making the check mark, and exchanging for desired items—and how they work together (in technical terms, the mechanisms).

Many of us have learned to self-manage. Even reading this book to reflect and change our parenting is a form of self-management. Science helps us figure out how that reflection and change can occur in reliable ways. Effective and compassionate interventionists learn the science and the principles so that all children in their care make reliable progress in big ways. The specifics, timing, and conditions to produce behavior change matter a great deal. A behavior analyst's knowledge of how behavior works, their problem-solving skills and wisdom, and their ability to collaborate for the child's benefit make the difference. Both parent and child are essential to the process that makes change valued and meaningful.

We know that our child will grow from moment to moment and from day to day. Even as an adult, they will grow and change. We can watch for those changes and respond to them. We watch for all the variations that come in our child's responses as well as shifts in their environment. We adjust to those changing conditions. Behavior analysts are trained to do this in sophisticated ways—that's what makes it a science. Parents don't have to be scientists to work with their child, but when they know enough about the science, they can make informed decisions about the actions that they, and the professionals, can take to make progress more rapidly.

We have explained only a few concepts with a few examples. And like all scientists, behavior scientists still have much to learn. Physicists devote years to studying the physical laws of gravity, a science that humanity has recognized only in the past 300 years. Physicists still have much to learn about gravity and our physical world. They learn more each year about these forces and how to use them wisely. It is the same with behavior scientists and the process of reinforcement.

Parents cannot be expected to know all this information, but they can expect the clinicians working with their family to know a lot about reinforcement and other concepts. Behavior analysts master a long list of foundational knowledge and skills. Clinicians should also be able to explain how the principles work, how the science supports the procedures they use, and the evidence that the procedures will be good for our child. Over time, as we work with well-trained behavior analysts, we will understand more about the principles that support the life we are building together with our child.

Evidence-Based Treatment

Science never solves a problem without creating ten more.
- George Bernard Shaw

Robust autism services start with keen understanding of a child's needs, deep knowledge of learning principles, and build on the best available research. Programs that approach intervention in this way are often described as evidence-based. In these programs, therapists and teachers tap their concern for the child, their experience, and their knowledge in order to adapt practices that show evidence of working in a research setting. Good evidence-based practice does more than follow a recipe of prescribed steps, however. For our child to make progress and feel loved, we must bring those steps to life with wisdom.

Experienced cooks know that a recipe in the hands of different people will turn out differently. The variety in baking and canning entries at a county fair, where all the participants are making the same thing, demonstrates this phenomenon. One popular contest even asks all the entrants to make a pound cake from the same recipe, using the same pan. Surprisingly, on contest day, the bakers bring cakes that vary widely in their appearance and taste.

How could that be? Many variables can affect the outcome of a recipe, such as the freshness of the eggs and the flour. Yet, even if you lined the bakers up in one room and outfitted them with all the same starting ingredients, the outcome would vary, reflecting every baker's preferences as well as their experience and skill.

A pound cake seems a straightforward recipe, one that is easy for many bakers to make, including beginners. However, more-experienced bakers might recognize that a pound cake has no leavening, such as baking soda or baking powder. They have had more practice creaming the butter and eggs together to get the maximum rise and lightest cake. They may also find that particular additions, such as almond essence or lemon zest, appeal to peoples' tastes or combine with other ingredients in a more satisfactory way. The classic chef's cookbook and reference *Larousse Gastronomie*, by Prosper Montagne, underscores what happens in every kitchen: the cook brings the recipe to life.

Similarly, in autism treatment, the interaction between our child's response and our response—the contingencies—bring a behavioral recipe to life. A behavioral recipe can start with a set of instructions designed to produce a particular outcome. In the best circumstances, an experienced behavior analyst or group of analysts have developed the instructions after working for a long time and under many different conditions.

With a behavioral recipe as a starting point (sometimes called a procedure, protocol, or treatment plan), a behavior analyst teaches a skill. The analyst then tests the success of that teaching under many conditions. They test from the easiest to the hardest conditions, checking the strengths and weaknesses of the recipe with each child. Like a great chef, a behavior analyst implementing a tried-and-true recipe then monitors our child's outcomes, to adjust the recipe to perfection.

The analyst also makes sure that whatever skill is being taught is relevant to our child. Learning a new skill takes a lot of time and energy.

To extend the cooking metaphor, we don't want to spend a lot of time preparing non-nutritious or dangerous foods that could hurt a child. Our child should learn skills that make a valuable difference in life.

Some good behavioral recipes have been developed in this way over the past few decades. In the best cases, scientific methods and review have shown the recipes, or protocols, to be reliably effective. Good practitioners have the knowledge and training to spot these useful recipes and adapt them; they have the skill and wisdom to bring a useful recipe to perfection.

Good practitioners can also take a recipe beyond the original instructions and combine it with other recipes in powerful ways. These practitioners not only recognize a decent recipe but also have a command of basic principles and technical skills to bring about excellent and valued behavior change. Just as every chef has favorite cookbooks and styles, good behavior analysts also have recipes that play to their strengths.

Most autism treatment manuals include a behavioral recipe for teaching a child how to imitate. Imitation may be the most important social learning we humans have at our disposal. Yet, because of the nature of autism, many children with autism don't learn to imitate others without being taught how to do so. When Sam was a toddler, Peggy saw early on that Sam didn't imitate her, so she couldn't elicit responses to help him learn. Not knowing what else to do, she started imitating his play to teach him, bit by bit, to imitate her. Since then, research has shown that what Peggy stumbled upon is a viable part of a series of recipes that lead to imitation.

To teach a child how to imitate others, Shahla uses some recipes from Ron Leaf and John McEachin's *A Work in Progress*, a manual used by many practitioners. When a good practitioner teaches how to imitate, a child with autism learns to imitate in all kinds of important ways, without extra help from others. When the teaching is successful, the child can and will want to copy what other people do, learning about the world from others. This is called generalized imitation in the technical vocabulary of behavior analysis.

So, what does it look like when our child is learning from a "master chef" to imitate other people? First, the practitioner will be an experienced, skilled behavior analyst who has been mentored by a master clinician to teach imitation to children with autism. The master teacher or clinician understood the research base and taught the practitioner the many intricate steps of the recipe. The practitioner will have read most of *A Work in Progress* and studied the instructions on teaching imitation skills. Each type of imitation (for example, imitating a word or sound, imitating a gesture or movement, imitating the clinician, imitating other children) has its own set of instructions.

Second, they all understand the program's conditions. To be successful, the practitioner continually adjusts their teaching to our child's circumstances so that their imitation skills occur in useful places. They will assess our child, talk to our family, and learn about our lives. They will know our short- and long-term goals. They will design a program just for our child.

Third, they will use their expertise to set conditions and deliver reinforcers to make imitation happen. In the best teaching, our child's imitation becomes generalized—our child learns to imitate like other children do, across all their environments and with the important people in their life. For example, when a friend shows off a new dance move, saying only "it goes like this," our child can imitate the friend's movement. Generalized imitation enables our child to imitate new words, write the alphabet, or use the toilet like everyone else.

A good practitioner will implement the intervention, monitor, and tweak the program until it works—until our child imitates others consistently, in novel and meaningful environments, and at the right times. In addition, our child and everyone around her will be happy with the program and the progress. After all, our child's ability to imitate others leads to other kinds of learning and their own path of discoveries.

Conversely, what does a poisoned recipe look like? The inexperienced, unskilled, or semi-skilled behavior analyst might have many problems along the way. Even when the practitioner takes a beautiful recipe from *A Work in Progress*, they can end up with a poisonous outcome because of poor conditions. Here are some of those conditions.

The practitioner had no mentor. A practitioner who hasn't seen the recipe modeled or the outcomes of a master practitioner is at a disadvantage. They have no idea what they are aiming for. They haven't witnessed dramatic change in a child. They don't know how the timing and sequencing of reinforcers work. Because they haven't seen success, they have no idea what is possible for our child. They have no one to imitate. Their expectations and our child's outcomes remain minimal.

The practitioner doesn't set up the environment for success. They don't understand the basics of motivation or how to arrange the teaching environment to work with our child. This can be hard to spot, but if we see therapists restraining our child in coercive and punitive ways or just letting our child wander, they probably don't know how to arrange an environment for learning. We all behave differently in different environments. Progress depends on what is required of us in each environment and how we feel about those requirements. That's no different for our child.

They start without an assessment of where our child is and the environment around them. They don't know our child's preferences, current skills, meaningful environments, or any of the possibilities for the child or the environment. Before designing a program that helps our child play with other children, for example, a skilled analyst will observe and know whether our child is looking and watching other children, whether they are approaching other children, whether they share interests and a play repertoire with other children, whether they can shift their play activities around other children, and more. The unskilled analyst, however, won't do this kind of assessment. They won't be able to select goals that are grounded in the child's needs. They won't start where our child is, and they won't take them where they need to go.

They won't assess the child across meaningful environments or work toward a graceful balance of changing the environment and the child for progress. Again, this may be hard to spot, but if our child is being taught with the exact same program as every other child, that's a troubling sign. In the worst cases, our child will learn ways to escape the subpar teaching situation, and some of those escape techniques can be disturbing or hurtful to their well-being.

They don't have the right support combinations. If the assessment is right, then our child will require increasingly less support to learn, and the help, such as prompts, can be removed. If what our child learned depends on eternal prompts, the recipe isn't working. In the example of learning to play with others, our child's foundation for learning stands on rickety stilts when the analyst must always recruit the other children and continually shift our child's play activities every time a play session begins. That said, the rules about prompts aren't hard and fast. A skilled person knows how to balance such potential dependencies with desired outcomes, weighing both with our child's well-being.

They are not responsive to our child. Almost everything about behavior analysis relies on observing the child's response—both their emotions and skills, followed by the clinician's impeccable timing and fluent responses to keep the happy learning going. If the practitioner does not have command of these techniques, they will get less-than-favorable results. Remember the baker who understood how to whip the butter, sugar, and eggs for the lightest pound cake? A behavior analyst with fine-tuned sensitivity to our child and deep understanding of reinforcement can use what they know to produce exquisite behavior change.

They don't make alterations or substitutions based on conditions. When conditions change from the protocol, they don't know how to change what they are doing, respond to our child differently, or alter the materials or the environment for success. They can't solve problems that emerge without warning or handle variations not accounted for in the recipe. A good cook who understands food chemistry and has sensitive taste buds can respond to conditions and make substitutions. When a good behavior analyst understands the mechanisms of behavior change, has seen strong outcomes, and loves happy learning, they will usually work to solve problems until they achieve progress. When an essential ingredient is missing, both the cook and the behavior analyst expect a bad outcome and know that they must adjust to a different recipe.

They don't have a community of both peers and masters to support their continuous improvement. A community that models new techniques, teaches new ways to apply principles, and finds shorter paths to success can make a big difference in professional expertise. Collaborating with another clinician to teach a child results in learning better, faster ways to teach. In Shahla's early career, she learned many fundamentals from her community of practice. She saw that progress was faster and more joyful when the team got together during the week to review progress, brainstorm, and solve problems. They learned how to adapt recipes to children's needs. She learned simple but important lessons from her community. For example, she learned that spending a half-hour every few weeks scoping out day care supply closets and watching the kids during their hour of free playtime made a significant difference for a particular child. Translating those observations, she then replicated toys and activities for imitation programs that the team was fashioning outside of playtime. This prepared the child for the time he spent with other children at the day care and for the road ahead.

They don't recognize that applied behavior analysis is a science, not a group of therapeutic practices. This concept confuses not only parents but also some therapists. Therapy is an interaction between a person who needs relief, healing, or help in improving and the person who guides the relief, healing, or help. A pill can also be therapy. Exercise is another type of therapy. In applied behavior analysis, therapy is a love- and science-based interaction where two or more people are engaged in an interaction. Their interactions change one another. A therapist acts and the individual responds. The individual acts and the therapist responds. The therapist reinforces that response or changes the conditions. If the individual doesn't respond as desired, the therapist must change what they are doing. Good program staff use their clinical knowledge of scientific methods, the principles of learning, their care for the child, and wisdom. They use proven research recipes, but they also gather evidence and data on their clients' emotional and behavioral responses, to evaluate and tailor their recipes, techniques, and tools.

Author and parenting expert Glenn Latham offered an elegant way to think about this need for continual adjustments. In *An Angel Out Of Tune*, he likened our parenting journey to a cross-country road trip listening to AM radio. As we pass through regions, we lose the frequency of the local stations. We keep our eyes on the road as we drive, but continually and responsively adjust the dial to stay in tune. Likewise, a skilled therapist continually adjusts to find the evidence and respond to our child lovingly and with flexibility.

This flexibility in the context of evidence-based treatment is key for everyone involved in our child's treatment. During autism treatment and beyond, parents, children, and therapists are learning how to have relationships with one another. Research discoveries won't do much good when deployed dogmatically or without kindness. Training in behavior analysis can help us be responsive as well as understand and maneuver the process. All of us can adjust our interactions without a lot of training just by keeping our primary goals in mind and by being responsive. When we learn that a softer dough keeps our cinnamon rolls tender, we'll watch for the right consistency and avoid adding too much flour. When we're listening for our child's first sentence, we'll be ready with an encouraging response no matter when we hear it.

While we are learning to be responsive, it's helpful to remember that we parents are often hard on ourselves, especially when we are tired, sad, or feel our patience wearing thin and are tempted to take a shortcut. We can exercise greater care when we are out of sorts, but we don't have to shame ourselves if we come up lacking, either. Shaming accomplishes little. We can coach ourselves to stop, reflect, and change when our child doesn't have the desired response. And we can rely on our connections and our community to help us.

We can make incredible progress with our child when we find solutions. Those solutions often require compromise, negotiation, and flexibility. This proves true in any human relationship, not just for the people closest to us. We aren't waffling or being inconsistent when we search for a context to resolve a conflict. In this way, parents are luckier than professionals, because we have the running start of loving our child. Love can make it easier to admit when we are wrong and need to make a change.

As we become more responsive, we will make new discoveries and learn new information. We can work to increase our child's access to high-quality interventions and supports. But easy answers will still elude us. Most answers come slowly and after great deliberation and care.

We can think about our child's whole life, their growth, and progress in new ways, confident that a detached, scientific viewpoint offers its own kind of love in what we choose to do. Each time we stop, reflect, and change our actions, we build a spiritual strength in our relationships. The more we shift course without rigidly adhering to a failing recipe, the more we adjust our actions to get the desired response, the more we move and change, the stronger we become and the more individualized and successful our recipes become. And that progress tastes sweet, indeed.

Unexpected Places to Find Wisdom

Resilience is all about being able to overcome the unexpected. Sustainability is about survival. The goal of resilience is to thrive.
- Jamais Cascio

Shahla had trouble with her clothes dryer for a long time. Every time it would go on the blink, she called the appliance company to send a technician. Then, the dryer broke down for good. She expected it, even though the dryer was manufactured by a company with a good reputation and the appliance should have had a longer life.

She bought a new, name-brand dryer that was on sale at a home improvement store. She liked how the new dryer looked. It was hip compared to the plain-looking units she'd owned before. When the new dryer began performing poorly, she went online. She knew Consumer Reports would have more-reliable data from their scientific testing about the dryer's performance, compared to crowdsourced information, but she read the customer comments anyway. Both indicated the dryer was not as good as it looked.

Then, the motor stopped working on the new dryer. A different technician came to fix it. Before making repairs, he asked Shahla a lot of questions. He didn't just want to know what had gone wrong with her new machine; he wanted to know the history of her old dryer's performance. That led him to the dryer vent. He discovered it wasn't built as it should have been. Because of that flaw, any dryer would run at higher temperatures than it was designed for and would have a shorter life. He took the time to study the whole system and made two repairs: one on the machine and the other to the vent. The new dryer continues to work well.

Shahla thought about what had happened. In this case, neither her understanding of the scientific reports nor the crowdsourced comments would have helped. When she called for repairs, she was handing off some of the responsibility for fixing what was going wrong in her home. The other technicians made a proper repair, but they didn't ask questions. Perhaps if she had shared her frustration with the recurring problem, another technician might have asked more questions about the vent. Or had she known more about how appliances worked and how her home was built, she might have been spared a lot of hassle and saved money.

The last technician proved to be an ally, one who brought not only the technical expertise Shahla didn't have but also a system-wide view to the problem. We don't know for certain, but maybe he grew up in a family with leadership values or the ethos of "do unto others." Or perhaps his company encouraged technicians to go the extra mile for customers, rather than reinforcing some other value in making repairs.

Likewise, therapists, teachers, and health professionals have trained in their disciplines. They can assist us when something needs to be addressed, such as toileting, trying new foods, improving sleep, or learning new words. But not all professionals can bring that deep, whole-system thinking to a problem the way that Shahla's talented appliance repairman did. Parents know their children and their family, which means they can bring deep understanding of the family's system when it's time to tackle a problem.

We parents know and understand our child and our family. We can explore our family's hopes and dreams as we develop priorities for our resources, as this, too, can deepen our understanding of our whole family system. For example, if we set up our child's daily life in a big schedule of "fixes," then we can put the integrity of our family system and our child's well-being at risk. Peggy and Mark had a long to-do list when Sam was a preschooler. During his free time, Sam's play didn't resemble the play of other children his age. He liked to turn toy cars and trucks upside down, spin the wheels, and stare at them for long periods of time. A few teachers and therapists called that activity "perseveration," not play. They advised the family to "extinguish" that kind of play at home. Mark and Peggy had already observed how much Sam's play evolved as he grew from a toddler to a preschooler, noting that his fixations changed. They decided that, as long as Sam was not hurting himself or anyone else, they wouldn't add "extinguishing perseverations" to their to-do list.

In one way, they were pragmatic. They needed to spend most of their time and resources helping Sam learn to talk in every possible way, which required far more time and attention than the weekly, half-hour sessions he received with a speech therapist. They spent time reading books, taking walks, and playing games that Sam liked. That crowded out some of the spinning activity.

It's also important to know that when Peggy and Mark were working through this issue in their own way, new lines of research were being developed that would have supported them. Marjorie Charlop and other researchers have since demonstrated that a child's intense interests can be used as a bridge to more conventional play. They are developing methods for expanding, rather than contracting, a child's interests. Peggy and Mark wondered whether Sam's odd play was useful for learning in some way that researchers were just beginning to understand, but they had no way to negotiate this with his teachers and therapists. What behavior scientists understand and what a family understands at any given point during autism treatment is fluid. That can be hard to tolerate for both parents and professionals who may want things to be more certain.

At the same time, these understandings can bring unexpected wisdom. Peggy and Mark decided that their children would learn about the world and express themselves through their play, however that might present itself. They worried that using their power as Sam's parents to stop his odd play would communicate a value they did not share—that they didn't like how he expressed himself. They were concerned that extinguishing how Sam expressed himself during play might affect their relationship in unexpected ways and push their parenting into a place of fear. Fear can be an adviser, but we must be aware of its grasp.

Sam didn't have distracting, unsettling, or dangerous habits as a boy. Some children with autism do develop those kinds of habits. Even in those cases, parents and professionals still must use care when addressing such behaviors—weighing the person's preferences, the potential harms, and the potential benefits in a child's life. Shahla worked with one child who preferred to spend most of his playtime on three activities, and in his case, all could be dangerous. Tanner liked to climb, using the kitchen appliances and the bookshelves for footholds. He liked to bang knives together. And he liked to crinkle cigarette paper. His preferences got the attention of family members, of course. But their attention also reinforced his preference for those activities and made it harder for everyone to make changes.

Rather than devising ways to eliminate Tanner's dangerous preferences, Shahla and the rest of the team studied them. Many children develop deep interests, such as identifying all the dinosaurs, memorizing breeds of dogs or horses, or collecting baseball cards. Children with autism also develop deep interests but often in a more restricted and sometimes unconventional range. The team recognized that certain sensations—the sounds and sights as well as the movements and feel of the activity—were important to Tanner. They devised ways to make the activities as safe as possible while allowing him to make the big movements and bold sounds he liked, particularly with clanking knives and crackling papers. The team used those activities as reinforcers for other important things he needed to learn. Soon, Tanner was climbing outside, playing Mr. Potato Head with his sister, and enjoying other activities that were less worrisome but that he still cherished. The foundations for family relationships were strengthened through Tanner's wider range of interests. As their efforts progressed, he considered many activities, such as riding a bicycle or swinging on the playground, to be enjoyable ways to spend his time.

When caring for someone who needs our help, we have known for thousands of years that it is important to first do no harm—the Hippocratic oath. On the one hand, we shouldn't extinguish behavior because we have the power to do so. We all, individuals with disabilities included, have the right to be ourselves and to do harmless things occasionally, like collect hundreds of paint sample strips or eat two box of crackers. On the other hand, parents also have the responsibility to create a healthy environment for the entire family, including encouraging new and expanding skills and fostering healthy relationships between each member.

We are obliged to care for one another. Our care must include a plan of action that considers the whole system around our child and their future. Without that, we are doomed to a series of breakdowns, never understanding why we have failed.

Sustainability

Sustainability is another word for justice, for what is just is sustainable and what is unjust is not.
- Matthew Fox

A biologist once approached a cattle rancher on the Red River about restoring habitat for bobwhite quail on the rancher's land. The rancher agreed but insisted that the work couldn't cost his operations in an ongoing way. The biologist knew that a healthy prairie would sustain the quail and the cattle, much as it had sustained the birds and roaming bison years ago. The rancher needed to spend a little money and energy to rebalance and restore conditions given that raising cattle the old way had led to the quail's decline. But for the long term, the rancher needed to direct the energy that he and the land already had, and in a way that maintained the prairie for both the birds and his herd without additional resources. The rancher's need for sustainability highlights an important lesson, for the research biologist and for all of us, about the value of sustainability.

When we think about supporting children in a sustainable way as they grow up, there are two important notions that are much like the rancher's concerns. First, all children require special care and education during their early years. Our autistic child who isn't talking or socially engaging with others will need different attention and require different resources, so we will put extra energy into getting things going early. The second notion is that we do this work in a way that encourages our child to gradually learn to direct their own life course. We work toward the dream of a happy, useful, and satisfying life.

Initial early intervention programs are comprehensive. These programs address all areas of our child's development. The main goal is to rapidly teach the critical skills that serve our child: how to communicate likes, dislikes, and interests; how to get along with others; how to learn by watching others; how to sample and engage with many different activities for leisure and to build vocational talents; how to make choices; and when and how to adapt. Our child won't completely master these skills before age five, as is true with any young child. But our child will be better served if we can establish the basics for learning as they move to advanced opportunities.

Some children may need comprehensive support for most of their lives, especially those living with other conditions. But children who bloom through a strong comprehensive program can increasingly sustain their own life. They don't require many additional supports. When they do, that work is often referred to as focused therapies. Many autistic children benefit from focused therapies as they grow, sometimes continuing into adulthood. This work may help them have clearer speech, strengthen their reading comprehension, or learn special skills, such as drawing anime characters, programming computers, or playing soccer or competitive Pokemon. The work is similar to the extra tutoring or coaching most children get as they show interests or a need for extra attention. That attention can sometimes come from mentors or community leaders and other times from professionals.

Comprehensive autism programs in the time of early research were successful because clinicians worked with the children across many domains. The programs were also swift, flexible, and responsive. Above all, they were effective. The effectiveness or lack of effectiveness drove the clinician's response. Clinicians added goals when needed and revised when needed, tackling hundreds of goals and objectives over a year's time. They focused on skills that would be valued in the child's future. They taught intensively, providing many learning opportunities throughout a child's day. They carefully broke skills down into pieces so that a child could acquire them successfully and with abundant reinforcement along the way. The programs were also carefully coordinated—the families, therapists, and teachers were on the same team, working for the child's benefit. The work left few gaps in time, place, or progress.

Currently, more families have access to care, and even more research is underway. New ways of paying for services could lessen the old disparities, regardless of where children live or how much money their family has. Research has shown that meaningful change can happen in many settings. Autism services are already big business in some areas, with treatment centers competing for a child's placement. With the right insurance, children may be offered many hours of clinic- or home-based therapy. In some cases, inclusive university lab schools or public schools offer specialized services, often for families without resources. Like the rancher, parents can remember this wisdom when considering their family's options: although it will take greater energy initially to create what is needed, the goal is a sustainable future. The process of imagining and building toward a better set of circumstances is something we all have in our capacity. We know from the research that the intensity of the work, the clinician's skills, and the coordinated efforts are important, no matter the setting.

To navigate the resource conundrum, then, we can remember that health insurance companies offer coverage through a business model. They work from the assumption that a disease or other pathology must be addressed. Their goal is to demonstrate medical progress and to end the treatment and payments. Working within this business model, behavior therapists must often "reduce a problem" or "remediate a deficiency" in a setting driven by funding. They are often prompted to design treatment plans that are focused, short term, and less likely to reflect the features of the early research.

The most caring and compassionate people will struggle to do good work under such conditions. A constricted setting and payment model can lead to rote, limited, and slow-moving treatment plans. We may sometimes ask too much even from experienced therapists in such constricted settings, let alone the therapists who are new to the job or the behavior techs who have had little time with master clinicians. Parents may find that they, too, are limited, with little information to help them participate in the progress.

Before we blame insurance companies, hospitals, universities, or treatment centers for this model, we must remember that we view them all as commodities, too. There is no easy resolution. In some cases, providers will find alternatives that don't compromise outcomes; in other cases, parents will develop alternatives. In the best cases, everyone wraps around the child and works the system together.

The most powerful, durable, and meaningful behavioral plans—even for the most challenging goals and problems—are "wraparound." These plans make the most of resources and options available and continually adjust the programs to serve the child's best interests. They arrange the conditions of a good life for a person and coach them into that life. The wraparound strategy requires a community, special training for at least some of the people using the strategy, and a good amount of attention and coordination among the parents and professionals involved.

For example, Tobias started his comprehensive program when he was three years old. His mother worked full time, and his grandmother brought him to and from the treatment center on the bus every day. The center had received a government grant to provide services to under-resourced families. The program included a social worker and master clinicians, but the subsidy funded just ten hours per week for Tobias, not enough time to build that initial boost of skills he needed. The family and clinicians didn't accept the limited options offered by fragmented and often broken systems of care. Instead, they combined their strengths and pieced together all the different systems to work in Tobias's favor.

The clinicians chose the learning goals with care. They concentrated on four areas: learning to learn, communication, social growth, and activity engagement. They did not let one minute go by without several learning opportunities and reinforcement. His grandmother watched every session at the center. The clinicians worked with his grandmother on how to translate his success at home. The day care at the family's church got involved, too. His afternoons at the day care were unstructured, but volunteers came to the center and learned what they could do to guide Tobias's new play skills and keep him happily engaged.

The social worker helped the family access an early intervention specialist through the school district. The specialist, in turn, helped the family find toys that suited his interests and the program goals. She visited the center and watched the master clinicians, and she learned how to better break down tasks for Tobias and to time the reinforcers so that he remained happy and progressing.

The master clinicians watched videos, shot on family smartphones, of Tobias with his many cousins. The cousins brought him into the fold with their weekend activities, giving the clinicians ideas for new things to include in their teaching. Through those videos, they could also see whether the clinic program was carrying over.

Over two years, Tobias mastered 200 objectives, which included imitating simple and complex actions, such as playing with Tonka trucks, talking in three- to four-word phrases, asking for things he liked and describing the things he loved, playing with his sisters and cousins, labeling useful and interesting objects and events, building complex structures of Legos, and telling his mother that he loved her. After that early, intensive, and comprehensive period, Tobias and his family made their way into the rhythm of education and some focused services, including reading comprehension and conversation skills with an after-school therapist a few times each week.

The types of focused services will vary from child to child, sometimes dramatically. For Lisa, a happy seven-year-old, the focused services required a bit more creativity. Her family recognized that their daughter was a budding artist. She also wanted to be naked all the time. Lisa was homeschooled, and her family wasn't bothered by Lisa's preference and worked around it, but she was also showing artistic promise. Her family knew that her talents, if developed, could open many doors, despite the severity of Lisa's autism. The reality was that, in order to receive art instruction, Lisa would have to learn to keep her clothes on. This was the focused goal: help Lisa be successful in art classes.

The team included behavior analysts funded through insurance and her family. They devised a gentle program to coach Lisa into the life she needed. Like all good programs, this one relied on Lisa's assent. She could walk away at any point that she was uncomfortable. She could be naked in her bedroom any time she wanted, and she could also take off her shoes whenever and wherever she wanted.

The first steps laid out choices for Lisa. If she wanted to come downstairs, she had to wear a leotard. If she wanted to go outside, she would have to wear clothes. Through reinforcement and adjustment based on Lisa's assent and communication, the program evolved until Lisa wore clothes whenever she was outside of her room. The program helped her team learn to respect her wishes, while at the same time working with her to find social boundaries and regulate herself within those boundaries.

During this period, Lisa was also learning how to find and select YouTube videos; how to imitate complex, fine motor movements; and how to sit for increasing amounts of time during that motor instruction. Each program wrapped around Lisa's needs in an individual way, working toward the goal of doing something she enjoyed that could develop into a vocation. What everyone on the team learned also propelled Lisa into an art class so that she could participate and benefit from the instruction. Her team learned to wrap around her strengths. Lisa developed a lifelong skill that suited her interests.

A good treatment program will inspire growth that our child and family can sustain and build upon. Some of the program will include figuring out problems, but the rest will include much construction: discovering interests and building new skills and repertoires. Over time, our child should respond with more self-sufficiency and autonomy. If a program or therapy requires the continued infusion of resources from our family or community without our child making progress, we must ask whether the work should go in another direction.

We increase our chance to create sustainable outcomes when we intervene early. The strongest intervention programs build habitats for our child that, as much as possible, lead to their own agency directing the course and circumstances of their life.

Attitude Matters

Battles are lost in the same spirit that they are won.
- Walt Whitman

At times, we won't have the information we need for our child and our family. If we remain open-minded when we are having problems, we can still make progress. When we have the right attitude, we are in a better position to see things clearly, ask questions, and find what we need to make good decisions.

Professionals are taught how to think through and solve problems in their specialty or discipline, whether it's botany, biology, or behavior science. We might defer to an expert when solving a particular problem, but we also know that no workplace, specialty, or discipline has a lock on the best ways to think through issues. We can borrow ideas from other professions and learn from each other to help keep our mind open and thinking clearly.

During flight school, for example, pilots go over problem scenarios. They learn to recognize a hazardous attitude in themselves through the choices they make to solve the problems. Pilots train to recognize those hazardous attitudes that can bring additional risk to the flight. After all, everyone wants to arrive alive. The pilots watch for attitudes that appear macho, impulsive, anti-authority, invulnerable, or resigned. With a little imagination, we can translate a pilot's problem-solving training to situations that we might encounter.

An example for this thought exercise might involve deciding what to do when a treatment program appears to be making little progress. The program is also draining our family finances. Our child has become frustrated and has started hitting people. A family member suggests to us that we should stop the treatment or at least get an outside opinion or another assessment before continuing. What would it look like if we responded with a hazardous attitude? If we tell our brother to "cool it" for butting in, we are showing a macho attitude. If we pressure the treatment center to increase the intervention because we are panicked and want the autism to stop, we are showing an impulsive attitude. If we decide that a second opinion or assessment is something a bureaucrat would dream up to waste our time and deny us resources, that shows an anti-authority bent. Yet, assuming nothing dangerous could happen to our child during treatment shows an invulnerable attitude. Or watching everyone become upset, including our child, but choosing to do nothing because we feel there's no use in changing the treatment now—that's resignation.

Some years ago, a news story in the *Chicago Tribune* examined chelation therapy and other dubious procedures that some practitioners were offering for autism treatment. In chelation, a child is given special drugs that bond with heavy metals to remove them from the body. The health care professionals using chelation did not call their treatment a cure for autism, but some families sought and defended the treatment as if a cure were possible. Readers commented on the newspaper story online. The comments illustrate various hazardous attitudes that can color parental and professional decision-making. Recognizing hazardous responses can be hard, but it's a first step.

Here are some examples:

The reporters "should be deeply ashamed of themselves for writing such a biased, ignorant article." (a macho response).

"The 'scientists' who lack the sense of urgency, intellectual curiosity, and moral courage to study and treat our kids are the ones who do harm. They, along with the writers and editors of this article who encourage their complacency, are accomplices in the death and destruction of our kids." (an impulsive response).

"My two-year-old son has autism, and he has a stronger sense of ethics in his beautiful, nonverbal little soul than any of these 'scientists' or government agencies that continuously seek to disprove methods of treatment that may not be tested by the elitist scientific community, but are tried and true to those of us waging this battle on a daily basis." (an anti-authority response).

"I'm right. I see that my comment was deleted by someone who is opposed to the truth. Chelation cures autism. No sane parent quits after just improving a few symptoms. We want our kids back to normal, the way they were born, before mercury mangled their brains." (an invulnerable response).

"Without money from the government or Big Pharma, there will be no research, and the scientific evidence so many people crave will not materialize. Parents are left to experiment on their children. Anecdotal evidence is better than no evidence in cases where the established medical community has nothing except behavioral therapy and psychotropic drugs to offer these children. Parents of autistic children are often desperate, and in desperation will experiment on their children. Sometimes these therapies result in real improvements, and sometimes there is no improvement, or the children regress. It's a sad situation, but desperate times demand desperate measures." (a resigned response).

In these cases, the parents' voices also flag the poor conditions that their families face as they try to sort through information and connect to others. When we are desperate, when we have little information, when we have no access to people with viable alternatives, who among us would not still try to solve our child's problems as best we can? In other words, the goal is not to extinguish an attitude but to recognize that the attitude signals a need for something more.

Shifting Toward Halcyon Attitudes

Be patient toward all that is unsolved in your heart ... try to love the questions themselves.
- Rainer Maria Rilke

Attitudes can give us cover from challenges we don't want to face, and can keep us from learning. Parents and professionals make better decisions when we are better aware of our attitudes. All children, not just those with disabilities, depend on the adults around them to keep them safe.

When we are in a tough spot, we can shift to identify poor conditions. Our perspective can serve as a source of strength, too, in making that shift. We can step back for a moment, ask ourselves a few questions, and study our responses to see whether our attitude is becoming a hazard to keeping an open mind and why this is happening.

Hazardous attitudes shift our focus toward falling. If we shift our focus toward rising, we can find a halcyon attitude, instead. The origin of the word "halcyon" is instructive here. Ancient Greeks spoke of a bird, the halcyon, that calmed the seas in order to build a nest to raise their young. Likewise, when we feel the chaos, we can pause and ask ourselves questions to calm the churning within so that our child can thrive. For example, am I worried about what other people think of me? What is it that that frightens me most about the choice in front of me? Do I recognize that the growth and development of every child, including mine, is worth my efforts and the efforts of others?

Our feelings don't lie. Fear and anger can forge a path to genuine understanding when we examine those feelings. One researcher who studies emotions, Jesus Rosales-Ruiz, points out that if we confront a bear in the woods and are afraid, we are not afraid of the bear itself. We are afraid the bear will maul us. Making that distinction helps us make better choices about what to do next, and increases the likelihood that we will act in a way that doesn't provoke the bear.

Creating that path for understanding also requires honesty on our part .

Who can blame us, for example, for being angry when people shame us for the decisions we make? They aren't walking our path. They don't know. Peggy had a confrontation with a well-meaning stranger during the year that Sam was finishing the second grade. Peggy brought Sam, and his little brother and sister, to an orchestra event that was more party than traditional concert. The event was a year-end tradition every spring. The setting was casual and a little noisy, as well as a good opportunity for all three kids to hear their father play his tuba in the orchestra. Concertgoers claimed seats around big tables set up in a large exhibit hall. They brought their own table decorations, food, and wine. The orchestra performed popular music, like movie scores and Broadway tunes. Given how young the children were (eight, five, and three years old), they behaved well through the entire concert. Sam had learned to stay in his seat, although it took him most of second grade to accomplish that goal (thanks to Kevin, Sam's teacher, and the aides). He fidgeted and stood next to his chair occasionally, but he didn't run around the family's table or any other people's tables during the performance.

One lady at a nearby table couldn't stop staring at Sam during the concert. The woman approached Peggy afterward. She started to tell Peggy what she thought was wrong with Sam. Peggy tried to be polite, but after a minute or two, she interrupted the woman and yelled at her. Horrified, the woman walked away without saying another word. Peggy was ashamed of losing her temper but also relieved. Judgmental strangers had been telling her what she was doing wrong as a parent for many years. In a certain way, she protected everyone's sense of accomplishment that day. The concert was a big success for Sam and the rest of the family. She wasn't going to let anyone else tell her otherwise. She forgave herself for yelling at the stranger by vowing—and keeping the vow—to be more gracious to strangers in the future, whether they were well-meaning or not.

We can look at our fear and anger in a constructive way, identifying both what we value and what we need to do next. When someone judges us, our feelings of shame can be a springboard to something deeper. We might be angry because we don't have the skills or the knowledge or the help to change things. When we don't get to read books, take walks, go out to dinner, or do other things we enjoy like everyone else, we may feel deprived. We feel the universe has dealt us a bad hand. We don't perceive that we have a choice. The grass is greener for others this time. Yet, there is other suffering in the world. Even our friends and neighbors are suffering—and in ways we may not know.

Researchers have studied human resilience to better understand the qualities that help us bounce back from a problem, keep our sense of self intact when facing difficulties, and calm our turbulent waters. We can be brave in a roomful of teachers, administrators, and lawyers when we ask for help with toilet training our child at home. We may suspect that they are judging our parenting skills—and we are right to some degree, yet many other people also care about our child. We know that our child needs help to make progress, and we have the right to ask for it. So we ask.

We can express our pain and let it go after it no longer serves us. We have a mountain to climb, and carrying our hurts with us can slow our progress like a bag of rocks on our backs. When we can reflect upon and forgive the sins of the day, we can wake the next morning free of the burden. So we climb.

Tragedy plus the passage of time equals comedy. We can keep our sense of humor, knowing we are making progress by seeing the bigger picture, solving the problems, and appreciating the struggle. So we can be happy.

Change is Intentional

The most difficult thing is the decision to act, the rest is merely tenacity. The fears are paper tigers. You can do anything you decide to do.
- Amelia Earhart

Each child is different, and that includes each child with autism. But research has found that no matter the differences in their autism, every child benefits from purposeful, high-powered experiences. We can intentionally consider everything about the changes that will happen during childhood, including where our child is educated, who educates them, what they need to learn, why they need to learn, and how much time we have as their guardians, protectors, and nurturers.

Perhaps we decide that our child would benefit most from a program at an autism center. Centers offer controlled surroundings with lots of one-to-one teaching. The model helps many children learn how to learn. Most autistic children benefit from having skills broken down and carefully sequenced to foster the development of new skills. To close that learning gap, we often have to work on basic things, such as how to gain attention, how to follow instructions to build an interesting toy, or how to watch a group and then imitate and join in the activities.

However, the strength that comes from teaching autistic children one-on-one in a controlled environment can also be a weakness. For example, the children may not take the imitation skills and other things they learned with the center's therapist and transfer them to more natural surroundings such as school and home, where they need to look to other children and adults to keep learning.

Perhaps we decide that our child would benefit more from receiving therapy and teaching while attending school with other children, some of whom are autistic and some of whom are not. If orchestrated well, the surroundings are more natural and richer with possibility. Our child can make progress in school and community settings. These settings come with so many built-in learning opportunities that we almost cannot count them all. These settings also come with weaknesses: the environment can be chaotic, the services uncoordinated, and the children can get lost.

Whatever setting we choose, we are better off being part of the team that is purposefully creating change. The team will consider, observe, count, and analyze our child's progress. If the progress slows, we want to know. We also want to understand the evidence about a setting's strengths and perils. Research shows that for our child to make progress, we all—teachers, therapists, parents, and sometimes even other children—must work with our child to stay engaged and remain responsive. This is key: we must transform many moments of the day, including our child's transitions from one activity to another, into intensive learning opportunities.

We can expect the people working with us to be overburdened. But we can help them, whether at a clinic, center, or school. We must help because an overburdened school or treatment center probably won't succeed without our vigilance and support. Treatment is an enormous undertaking. Great outcomes are possible, but so are frightening ones if we stop assessing and planning ahead or allow ourselves too many shortcuts. By keeping the big picture in mind as we make small decisions along the way, we can stay on track.

Achieving purposeful, high-powered interactions takes work. We can expect the professionals in our child's life to be honest with themselves about whether they have the skills to do so. We parents have skills of our own. Both parents and professionals can improve the skills that make interactions more purposeful, while shaping decisions to ensure that the work proceeds with care.

Parents can start in simple settings with basic interactions and move to more complicated ones as their skill and confidence grow. For example, we can join our toddler as she plays with a toy train on a wooden track and respond to the words or sounds she makes as she plays. We are careful to notice how she enjoys our attention and interacts with us as she plays. We adjust the timing of our actions to her responses. Over time, we analyze the words and sounds she uses and then devise new responses to encourage more words and phrases from her as she plays.

A skilled therapist who is able to count and analyze our interactions with our toddler can help us move from simple interactions to complex responses that foster her growing vocabulary. This kind of progress is possible within and across many settings, including clinics, schools, and homes. Shahla worked with researchers Kristin Guðmundsdóttir and Gabriela Sigurðardóttir to develop a telehealth program for rural Icelandic families. The families work with their children to increase the frequency and complexity of interactions, an intervention that has gained strength over the last decade. The work empowers families to accomplish goals that once seemed inaccessible and to do so at home, the setting that makes the most heartfelt difference for a child.

After each interval of purposeful interactions—for example, our child's play and expressive vocabulary—we can stop and take stock again. We can observe what has happened over the hour, week, month, and year. We should ask ourselves whether our child's life is better, and ask our allies whether they agree. Once we have those answers, we can think about the future, decide what's next, and how to move toward it.

Sam made great progress with speech programs at home and at school throughout his elementary years. During a planning meeting in middle school, his speech therapist announced that Sam was proficient enough to pass the speech assessments designed to detect most language deficits in children with autism. However, she added, Sam's language skills still needed work, and everyone around the table agreed. She proposed a different assessment and planned a new program for Sam. They would work on his abstract language skills, such as analogies, idioms, metaphors, and the like.

The team was enthusiastic. The focused work paid off.

A few years later when Sam was in high school, Peggy and Sam happened to be driving through downtown Fort Worth when a billboard in Spanish caught their eyes. Both Peggy and Sam had studied Spanish, but Peggy didn't understand what the billboard was saying. Sam told her, "that's because it's an idiom," and then translated the Spanish into an approximate English idiom for her. Combining rich scenarios with high-powered, purposeful interactions can transform the possibilities for individuals with autism. Moreover, there are thousands of possibilities as varied and unique as the individual. (Learning the concepts of idiomatic speech was just one such possibility for Sam.)

We can affect the direction and quality of our child's transformation into adulthood through the opportunities that life hands us and the choices we make. We search for kind, effective, and joyful ways to make changes. Some choices will have far-reaching consequences. The choices and consequences may change the opportunities we have, the people we connect with, the parts of the world we experience, and the amount of joy or suffering that we feel over the course of our lives. Jesus Rosales-Ruiz and Donald Baer offered a concept of human development describing how humans change and grow over time, in ways that don't always happen in a linear, stair-step fashion. They suggested that change can come in more transformative ways.

The interactions between what we do and our environment (contingencies) can lead to a revolution in how we experience the world. Sometimes changing the environment brings revolutionary changes. Sometimes learning a simple thing quickly opens new experiences and multiplies the possibilities, such as a young child learning to imitate or an adult with autism discovering the difference between seeing a basketball game on television and attending in person. A new relationship can also bring many wonderful changes and opportunities for our child and our family, such as meeting another mother with lots of good advice (changing the possibilities open to our child) or a new neighbor who is ready to step in as a surrogate grandmother (providing a new source of love and learning, respite, and so much more).

This process of development is called a behavioral cusp. The outcome of a change in the person or the environment produces a transformation, moving from one way of experiencing the world to another, profoundly different way of experiencing it. The concept of cusps is important to intervention because rather than thinking of change as something that happens bit by bit, we can focus on transformative changes that are more likely to save precious time. Cusps also prompt us to think about both the particulars and the whole: our child, their future environments and possibilities, and their responses, strengths, and interests over time. In doing this work, we also have to consider what is important.

We might think of a behavioral cusp as similar to major advances in computer technology, as educators Garnett Smith and Patricia Edelen-Smith do. The smartphone, for example, displaced many technologies by putting a small computer in our hands. That computer connects us to the rest of the world in more ways than a telephone did. Cloud services, as another example, are displacing CDs, DVDs, and even live television, changing how and when we access media and information. Those changes have changed how we interact with the world in important and expansive ways. Smith and Edelen-Smith encouraged interventionists to use the concept of the cusp to advance an individual's connections to the world around them in purposefully powerful ways. Cusps lead to experiences and skills that are important to the individual and their family, now and in the future. Cusps help construct a whole new way of life, with more choices, connections, and relationships.

Learning to imitate is perhaps among the most powerful behavioral cusps for young children with autism. As infants, children without autism mirror their parents, caregivers, and siblings. As they grow, their ability to observe and copy others creates a momentum that allows them to learn even more from the world around them. It allows a child to know the joy of learning a fun dance move by copying a friend when they say, "do this!" and demonstrate. At some point, they also discover the concept that imitating others isn't always appropriate, usually about the time someone in their life pleads "stop copying me!" A child's failure to imitate others is part of diagnosing autism. In purposefully teaching imitation, we open a child's world and this can be a behavioral cusp. Imitation involves watching what is happening, seeing what people do, and doing what is observed so as to access good things and continued learning.

Shahla worked with one little boy, Liam, who loved fishing lures. He had tackle boxes full of them. Liam enjoyed holding and stroking the lures. He always kept one or two in his pockets. Shahla and the team saw that

Liam's affinity for lures made it possible to teach him how to imitate. Bringing the lures to the intervention was a cusp; it opened up possibilities for teaching and for learning to imitate. Both are potentially cuspal.

The team approached their analysis and treatment plan with compassion, since not every fixation makes a ready platform for a child with autism to learn imitation. They first showed Liam that they were trustworthy and that they weren't going to take his lures away, as others had done in the past. No child can learn when they are distressed, worried about losing what they love most, freaking out, and in survival mode.

The team brought their own tackle box to their sessions with Liam. The tackle box had several awesome lures inside. They offered their lures to Liam during the sessions, but he also had to give them back and share. To start teaching imitation, the therapist made a game of taking a frog lure and play-jumping it into a bowl of water. Liam had his own bowl of water and did the same with his own lure.

Then, the therapists expanded Liam's imitation skills to body movements, mouth movements, and speech sounds. These activities improved his language skills, which still consisted of some echolalia. Echolalia is a term for the repeated speech patterns common in young children learning to talk that sometimes lingers with autistic children. After a while, the team expanded Liam's program to include other children, so that his observation and imitation skills could be guided, eventually expanding those skills in natural, sustainable ways. He began to interact and learn from the other kids and from his teachers in the day care.

In terms of the design of Liam's intervention, two important openings happened that were intended to be cuspal: Shahla and the intervention team respected his interests to teach him, opening new doors for learning, and what he learned opened new doors for relationships.

We can watch for cuspal experiences throughout our child's life and nurture those transformations. As Sam prepared to graduate high school, he joined the team to plan his transition to community college and the working world. The planning came with a dilemma over resources: he could get either state support for attending college or support for getting a job, but not both. By opting for job support, Sam could access coaches who worked with him to find and train for a job. The support also included time with a trainer to prepare for his driver's license exam. Counselors could work with him again in a new job search if he ever got laid off, or when he graduated from college later and was ready to look for a better job.

However, Peggy didn't see what other support Sam might need after he got his first job until an old family friend and colleague of Shahla's pointed it out. Don Louis's expertise was in vocational rehabilitation, a discipline that evaluates people's job skills and works with them to find a new line of work or get back to work after an injury. Don told Peggy that she would be surprised at how much Sam would grow and change after he started his first job. Learning to be successful in a new job means scores of new skills, choices, connections, and relationships, he said. Learning all that would lead to other opportunities.

Don's wisdom triggered a flood of memories for Peggy: how much she had to juggle between her part-time jobs and her school work and how different it was to work full time than to cobble part-time jobs in between high school and college studies. She'd almost forgotten how overwhelmed she felt after starting her first full-time job, including how tired she was at the end of the day those first few weeks. Peggy reconnected with those experiences and was ready to work with Sam so that he could understand and grow from his experiences, rather than be bewildered by them.

Peggy didn't know that Don was describing the possibility of a behavioral cusp for Sam. But Don knew it was important to give her a heads-up on both the flood of changes and the possibilities. By doing so, Don helped Peggy and Sam construct a whole new way of life that gave Sam more choices, connections, and relationships.

Both Liam and Sam underwent a metamorphosis. Their teams intentionally changed the environment in ways that expanded their worlds and accelerated their development into adulthood.

Considering the problems with being a caterpillar, it might be easy to be afraid and just focus on the dangers that can beset the tiny creature, rather than the needs for becoming a butterfly. Fear is a tricky friend. Fear means we need to do something. If we stay with our fear, we'll be in survival mode. If we detach from that fear, at least a little bit, we can take stock, consider why we are afraid, and think about what to do next. The cusp encourages us to think about what could be and the environments that might facilitate a healthy progression into adulthood. We expand the possibilities and imagine new paths and ways to work with our child to communicate the need for a reprieve.

When we think of cusps as a process of bringing about metamorphosis, we might also better see how to shape the environment and in doing so, offer our child more powerful agency in the future.

Learning to Learn

Love people. Cook them tasty food.
- Penzey's Spices

᛫ᛟ

Food plays a big role in the way we connect to family and friends. It also presents many opportunities to apply what we learn and build new skills as we work with our child. We bond over meals that we cook together and eat together, whether we're baking and sharing birthday cake, tailgating before the big game, breaking a fast together, or assembling tamales for the holidays. Meals often mean more to us than simply consuming the food we put on our plates.

We may admonish ourselves not to link food and love—ostensibly for fear of drowning our sorrows in butter or chili con queso—but food and love remain connected. We celebrate many occasions with family, friends, and our favorite dishes. When we are sick, or someone we love is sick and suffering, or when a loved one dies, we bring food to bring comfort. Choosing food, preparing food, bringing food, serving food—these acts show how much we care for one another.

Many autistic children and adults are selective about what they eat. If our young child is picky, we worry about how they are growing and developing. We also worry about their long-term health no matter their age. In addition, our child may miss out on building those many loving connections that seem to come without effort as family and friends share a meal together.

Picky eaters create other dilemmas for a family. How can we enjoy dinner in a restaurant or as a guest at a friend's house when there's nothing on the menu for the picky eater? If we accommodate our child's limited choices, are we being unfair to our other children if we don't also accommodate them? Yet, if we allow ourselves to become short-order cooks, what value does that communicate and reinforce in our family? Or if we limit the menus for the entire family, what then?

Sam usually ate a kid-friendly version of whatever Peggy or Mark prepared until he was three years old and began refusing food. Most often, Sam refused a food or a whole category of foods after something on his plate surprised him. Sam refused pancakes, French toast, waffles, and any other home-cooked breakfast foods after biting into a pancake that still had a bit of batter in the middle, for example.

In addition, Sam began vomiting in the middle of the night, triggering an aversion to the foods that had upset his stomach. Over several months, his food choices narrowed further until he refused everything except commercial breakfast cereals. By age four, he ate only cold cereal with milk for breakfast, lunch, and dinner. Peggy and Mark agonized that something about Sam's health was going undiagnosed. They worried that he would become malnourished and suffer in his growth and development. Sam's doctors had nothing to offer. Seeing that they were on their own, the family made a concerted effort over more than a decade to reintroduce foods and restore Sam to a varied, healthy diet.

Because food means so much to our well-being, our family, and our culture, learning how to work with a selective eater is an excellent way to apply what we are learning and build new skills. If we learn to shape our world and our child's world to make progress at mealtime, we will discover that we can tackle a lot—a potential behavioral cusp for both parent and child.

As science advances, researchers have begun to distinguish what affects children who are selective about food from children who have physiological difficulties with food. The treatments are different in each case. Research is increasing our understanding of how to shape and expand food choices for selective eaters. At first, therapists would not allow children to refuse what was offered, eventually triggering their acceptance of new food choices. Those picky eaters were force-fed, in other words. In extreme cases, therapists force-fed by holding a spoon to a client's mouth until it was accepted. This is a short-term fix and one that, if not carefully managed, can lead to aspiration pneumonia. Force-feeding presents other risks as well. A child who is force-fed may decide that other things about the treatment are scary. If the therapist force-feeds with a spoon, for example, that child might develop a fear of spoons. One of Shahla's clients howled each time his family drove by the hospital where he was force-fed.

Force-feeding only prevents a child from escaping food. The technique doesn't help them approach food willingly. We can't expect force-feeding to move our child toward an important, long-term goal for mealtime: happily joining friends and family at the table and eating what is served.

Therefore, how we set up the entire environment around our child's food choices becomes vital. A good program can help a picky eater expand the types of food they will eat. Shahla worked with a large team comprising clinical staff, Jesus Rosales-Ruiz, and a graduate student, Joe Cihon, to develop one such program, Yummy Starts. The team worked with many different children who found food unpleasant, even noxious. When a child refused to eat, the team didn't see that as a compliance problem. Instead, they observed the child's reaction to food. They discovered that the reactions resembled other phobias: a fear of heights, small spaces, loud sounds, or tarantulas. To design a program, they kept in mind how to best work with autistic kids who were afraid, in part by using research from their own lab and the research of Robert and Lynn Koegel and Daniel Openden. This work taught them that gradual exposure was critical. They also knew that in order to make progress and to build up new behaviors, they must start with many choices and things that kids enjoy. They also knew that to build new behavior with strength and resilience, interventions work best.

They grounded their work in an important 1972 study by Martha Bernal. She worked with a four-year-old girl and her mother on how to make changes at mealtime. The parent and professional collaborated on a series of steps that helped the little girl eat an ever-increasing variety of foods. They made the most of her preferences, which included soft and sweet foods, along with a few television programs. They used these preferences to reinforce the girl's efforts both to feed herself and try new foods. They worked systematically and were sure to reinforce each attempt the little girl made, which boosted what she would try and eat. Over five months, the girl had quadrupled the number of foods that she would eat and seemed to enjoy most of the foods her family ate.

Bernal's groundbreaking work showed how scientific developments opened possibilities for changing behavior in systematic and comfortable ways, without force. If our child is eating only breakfast cereal, we can build a program that shapes his enjoyment of a greater variety of healthy foods. We have dreams of seeing our child sitting and eating with the family at dinner, or with other students at the school lunch table, or as an honored guest at another family's Seder. Our child is part of our social community, with traditions for connecting, and food is often a big part of that. If our child joins others at the table and happily samples something new, then we've entered a cusp.

Our child's goals, then, are being receptive to sampling foods, gathering with the people they love to share those foods, and building healthier bodies. We work with our family and community to understand those goals. Together, we figure out the responses and environments that will help our child remain happy as they eat and remain engaged as best they can with the people around them. There will be technical work to achieve that. We will present all kinds of fruits and vegetables, mixed and separate, and prepared in the myriad ways they might be prepared in family culture. We make mealtime pleasant. We are happy at the table. Over time, we show that approaching meals and food with enthusiasm is part of life's joys. As we go along, we observe our child and collect the data to make sure that not only are we making progress but that it is happy progress.

To develop Yummy Starts, Shahla and the team started with the children's physical assessment. Physicians evaluated the children for allergies and physiological problems, since the way to approach food in such cases will be different. The team studied what each child ate willingly, and then, before determining the next steps, watched the child's response to new food choices. They focused on large classes of foods and the child's responses to food. Does he prefer crunchy foods over soft foods? Salty or sweet? Does she reject the food when she sees it on the plate, or will she try it first?

The team interviewed family members and listened to their concerns. They asked about immediate and long-term goals for the child and family. How and what does the family eat now? When and where? What do they want their child to enjoy and share with the family? In those talks, the team unearthed goals, potential resources, and support for change.

The staff worked with one family who followed halal for meals. Over time, a strange thing had shaped their family mealtime: their son, Sina, ate only chicken nuggets. The family loved Sina and did what they could to make sure he ate something every day. Each afternoon, they went to the local drive-thru to pick up the nuggets. The kind restaurant owners would even have them ready.

A program to eliminate Sina's preference might seem reasonable: chicken nuggets were neither very nutritious nor always halal. But such an action presents risks. When we use aversive techniques to stop our child from doing something, we risk our relationship with them as well as giving rise to our inner demons. If we spank our child in anger, we know we are usually responding to our own discomfort, shame, or fears. Even when we are more sophisticated—using time out, for example—little good comes of only trying to stop a behavior. We often resort to punishment when we lack the skills and ability to build something new.

Sina's affinity for chicken nuggets was not a weakness; it was a starting point. The team and his parents understood that. They could use Sina's preference to build new food preferences and expand, rather than contract his world. For example, Sina enjoyed the crispy coating of the chicken, which helped to shape his acceptance of similar choices, such as crispy-coated meats that his family prepared within their dietary guidelines. Eventually, he moved onto falafel and coated vegetables mixed with rice.

At the dinner table, there are many things going on all at once and over time. That stream of activity makes up all the contingencies in the environment we call mealtime. When we understand that stream of activity and rope off pieces of it to contingently shape the environment for our child, we can use those conditions to help our child expand their food choices.

Contingency is a common word, but it has a specific meaning for behavior analysts. The world moves in time and events happen in time. Behavior analysts look at the environment and all the stimuli in the environment to understand the relationships of events in time—the contingencies. They understand and test contingencies as a series of "if-then" relationships. They think about future probabilities of behavior when they examine the contingencies around it. Then, they arrange the contingencies in the environment to make a behavior more likely to occur. In Sina's case, the contingency was to try bits of the new coated foods his mother prepared and then eat some of the nuggets.

To begin their process with each child, the Yummy Starts teams set up short play sessions about thirty minutes before mealtime. The dining sessions came later and lasted only as long as the child desired, often no longer than ten minutes. The therapist invited the child to come to the lunch room with them, and the pair sat at a table with two plates of the same foods.

The therapist (and the parents, as the program involved them, too) interacted with the food and talked with the child. They made mealtime a happy place. They thought about and researched how they could set up the best conditions for success. Nothing surrounding the time together with food was coercive in any way. If the child pushed away the plate of food, they allowed and welcomed the child's opinion. The program involved the child's complete assent. The children were able to walk away from the table whenever they needed or wanted, up to and including not going to the lunchroom with the therapist at all. The therapist knew they had to establish a relationship with the child that was honest, responsive, and fun. The child's assent was critical for the team to know that each child was approaching the mealtime with happiness and without force. The child's dissent was a signal to change what they were doing.

Therapists made sure to work with a wide range of food choices and rotated the sets of foods frequently. They made sure there were several choices on the plate that the child liked, including at least one choice they relished, such as nuggets for Sina.

The goal foods, full of balanced and healthy possibilities, sat among many choices on the plate. For example, if the child liked crunchy foods, lunch might include carrots sticks and apple slices along with a few whole grain crackers. This gave the child more choices and the therapist more opportunities to reinforce.

The team made the plates look appetizing. Moreover, if the child refused something one day, the team didn't force the child to empty the plate or wrap up the food to try again the next day. Working on the same sandwich four days in a row is not a happy opportunity for anyone.

Having the therapist eat the food was part of the program, not only to model happy eating, but also for them to feel and taste the contingencies, so to speak. No one wants to waste food, but appetizing choices matter. To achieve success, they also tapped their personal qualities, embedding social affection in the interactions by responding to each child with love and enthusiasm.

As a result of the carefully planned and orchestrated contingencies, children began sampling the food on their plates without distress. Success comes when a child tries the new food, and each attempt at sampling results in a piece of their highly preferred food. The perfectly timed reinforcer in the midst of all these conditions is important. With each reinforced sample, the therapist reacts with enthusiasm. This becomes part of the reinforcer package. With each child, the team was reliably able to serve plates filled with more-complex food choices and that offered chances for exploration.

The children might not eat everything on the plate, but they tried a bit of everything. The children's data showed that if the teaching was skillful, the children would sample each new thing faster and more happily over time. The best moments came when they looked expectantly at the adult's face during a new taste experience and laughed when it was enjoyable for both of them.

While our child's main goal may be trying more foods, we have another important learning goal in this work: to increase the ways we learn to reinforce our child's efforts. Both food and social affection and attention are a part of mealtime. Supporting a picky eater to make more food choices by offering foods at just the right time and the right quantity is an important first step. But when we find shared appreciation in a delicious peach or our child shows that they feel the warmth of our smiles, laughs, hugs, and other social interactions, we are in the process of expanding our relationship and our child's social world.

Sometimes our child's food preferences can also be used to expand other learning opportunities beyond mealtime. But such work must be done with care. There is something wrong, on many levels, if instructors rely on bulk purchases of colored candies and fish crackers to sustain any child's behavior. At the same time, using coercion or threatening responses are poor options to bring about change. But that doesn't mean we resign to a lesser goal. Sometimes therapists choose arbitrary consequences (not related to the response or the setting) to jump-start a behavior or teach the prerequisites. In other words, a few treats may be there in the beginning until therapists can arrange natural consequences related to a response and setting to make progress. Choosing reinforcers is complicated. A master analyst knows where to start and how to progress so that, in the best circumstances, results come via the most natural consequences—those similar to what other children and adults experience in that setting. Knowing how to do this as naturally as possible is a super skill, in which master analysts often shine.

Food programs such as Yummy Starts can lay the foundation for us to find and nurture more-natural and social reinforcers for our child. We can make progress as we systematically expand our child's preferences. (That's another super skill of master analysts—understanding and respecting a child's preferences and how to expand those preferences quickly.) No matter the environment—the dinner table, playground, clinic, or school—our work with our child establishes new experiences for all of us, and our child's reinforcers can become less arbitrary. We learn to understand and expand our child's preferences and create more opportunities for us and our child to learn and experience more of the world.

We want our child to come joyfully and eagerly to each learning situation. We want them to trust that there will be the right reinforcement and timing for them to do so. Our child needs to learn to do what parents, teachers, doctors, and therapists ask of them. Over time and with effort, we hope they will be motivated by many of the social and tangible consequences that we all share. We also hope that most of those consequences will be based on positive reinforcement contingencies and involve a circle of people who care for them and foster their continued growth.

We do this knowing that human patterns of responding and learning are complicated and not limited to particular types of positive reinforcement. Behavior analysts go through years of training to learn these principles and how they translate to intervention. Their super skills include understanding other variables like negative reinforcement, positive and negative punishment, stimulus control, stimulus discrimination, and generalization. What parents know about the specific ways that their child responds to the world—what they like and don't like—makes them important partners in that process.

There's one more dimension to keep in mind: as we work with our child to expand their preferences, we also want to honor their unique presence as they move out into the world. Consider Mitsue, who was interested in lightbulbs far more than most other four-year-olds were. When he entered a room, he noted how many lightbulbs were in the room. He announced how many were burned out and needed to be replaced. Mitsue's speech was also limited. Using researcher Marjorie Charlop's work as a guide, Shahla and the rest of the team started with his uncommon interest in lightbulbs, to expand his world. Mitsue may have been consumed by thoughts of lightbulbs, but the team found ways to respect it. They worked with him in learning about the kinds of lightbulbs: incandescent, fluorescent, LED. They worked with him to learn how lightbulbs get their energy from electricity. When Mitsue worked with the team to build a house of toy blocks and outfitted that little house with toy LED candles, they were building his bridges to the rest of the world. These bridges allowed Mitsue's communion with and learning from everyone else, while still finding a place for his love of lightbulbs.

Honoring our differences while still honoring the human collective seems to be the struggle of our times. Being different doesn't mean being wrong. We each find our own place, yet we still bridge to everyone else. For some autistic children, the learning obsessions can become a vocation. An individual talent for precision and depth can be stunning and beautiful in the workplace or community. Figuring out how to be comfortable around people who are different from ourselves is a big learning opportunity for all of us. When we learn the lessons in what moves us in our relationships, we see that there is room for lots more variation than we might have believed at first.

We all want friends and we all want to be a friend. Our family and friends will keep moving through life, helping our child experience things that widen or change their interests and even their abilities. There will be many opportunities to learn.

We are starting to trust in a future that we don't know and can't see. When we fill our child's programs with the technical skills, care, and regard that we know our child deserves, when we imbue the program with our family's deepest-held principles and values, when we ensure the program follows what our child values in life, we build in progress and success. We are learning.

Part Two: The Power of Connecting

When we give cheerfully and accept gratefully, everyone is blessed.
- Maya Angelou

❧

No parent raises a child alone. Yet, there are times when parents feel alone, particularly parents of children with disabilities. We feel we are asked to be not only a parent but also a teacher, a speech therapist, occupational and physical therapist, behavior analyst, medical researcher, nurse, case manager—our child's everything.

Family, friends, and professionals can work with us. We can also benefit from the wisdom of others who have gone before us. These connections can make a difference in helping our child's progress, and outshine what we alone can do. As alliances and collaborations, our connections to others can contribute to raising a happy child and to making our adult life happy, too.

When we understand the connections between us, we can make the most of our relationships with other people. We can recognize a captain among our collaborators, that professional who deserves the trust to lead alongside us parents. We can identify the people capable of locating the right path for our child—the scouts. We can also see the vanguards, those extraordinary individuals, whether parent or professional, who are capable of moving a child through uncharted territories.

In this section, we share stories of families surrounded by and connected to others who respect and reflect their values, demonstrating a power that gives children more opportunities to learn. To make progress, our child needs caring, wise, purposeful, intentional actors in their life. Connecting to friends, extended family, and other parents also fosters shared wisdom. Parents and professionals can collaborate to make progress. While this work may seem magical, in this section we offer a closer look at these generous connections, which often share qualities such as reciprocity, resilience, and learning from one another. As we figure out what works and doesn't work in relationships forged around our child, we can make the most of one another's strengths. We may find ourselves trading a mediocre bedside manner, figurative or literal, for great surgical skills, since that is sometimes good enough to make progress. We can also be observant and alert to avoid the land mines that can erupt in any relationship from time to time. We can find ways of sharing the burden of deciphering large amounts of information and advice. For those uncommon situations when someone proves not to be an ally, this section offers information on how to handle that, too.

Finally, this section offers ways and places to find connections in the community, where belonging can boost loving relationships and contribute to everyone's feelings of well-being and happiness. Connecting to others helps families find wisdom and meaning in what may otherwise seem like chaos. This is the collective wisdom that helps power learning and loving.

Reciprocity Fosters Connections

Let us always meet each other with a smile, for the smile is the beginning of love.
- Mother Teresa

৶ৡ

Reciprocity, the ways in which we demonstrate our care for one another and influence and depend on one another, breathes life and depth into our relationships. Mutual dependence is part of the human experience. The most meaningful relationships might start by attending the same class, then remembering birthdays or taking turns buying lunch, eventually deepening over the years by sharing child care or stepping in when someone starts cancer treatment. Reciprocal interactions with family and friends not only nourish our lives but can also help our autistic child by creating healthy and natural dependencies that bring progress in a sustainable way. When we understand and value reciprocity, we can boost its practice and our family's quality of life.

Consider how young children learn to play together, for example. A child without autism approaches another child at preschool who is playing with cars, but just by watching the action at first. Then, the child picks up another car and begins playing along. After a minute or so, the two children create together an imaginary scenario for the cars. The play then becomes a learning, rewarding experience for both of them. That is one key of reciprocity—it is founded on mutual reinforcement. Each person receives some benefit in the relationship. The benefit may be transactional, meaning that something immediate happens that both parties value. The benefit can also be relational, meaning that things happen over time that are important to both individuals, and the value occurs when they are together. Reciprocity also involves coordinated and shared attention. Each person finds happiness in the other person's happiness.

Many of us, including our children with autism, struggle with reciprocity, especially in the beginning. To create a shift, some behavioral programs teach a child to ask, "Do you want to play?" However, unless a child is setting up a board game or similar activity, few children initiate play this way. Imagine the previous scenario with the toy cars, and now imagine our child with autism approaching the two children busy playing with cars and asking "Do you want to play?" The other children may see our child's request as a welcome interruption and a chance to expand their play. Or they may not. If the other children don't welcome the change, they aren't necessarily being mean. They, too, are learning about reciprocity in their own growth and development.

Consider the circles of people around us who make our life better. For most of us, family and close friends make up the inner circle. Groups of friends from spiritual communities, social clubs, or sporting activities are in the middle. The outer circle is filled with our acquaintances and professionals, such as our barber, school counselor, or family doctor.

The guidance counselor in Sam's elementary school, Michael Ball, thought a lot about the friendship circles among the schoolchildren. The students with disabilities, he knew, would have a hard time developing friends for their inner circle from that middle circle of friendships. To change that environment, he created many circles of friends, inviting Sam or another student with a disability into his classroom once a week along with several children without a disability to spend time together. He offered the circle of friends an activity they would all enjoy. He was careful to pick something that Sam or the other children with disabilities could do with some success, yet something all the children would enjoy doing or playing. Then, he'd let things unfold, working with them to solve problems along the way, if needed.

Researcher Mary Baker structured this kind of approach by creating games that both children with autism and their siblings without autism could enjoy. She watched the sibling groups before, during, and after her intervention. Not only did they play together more after the intervention, but they also looked measurably happier and started varying the ways they played together.

Children with autism often need coaching or other guided practice to take part in basic reciprocal social interactions, such as playing with siblings at home, with friends on the playground, or at a birthday party. Other children with autism may only need priming or a special script that details what happens and how best to respond to basic social cues. Some children may also need to expand their interests so they have more to share and can find common ground with family and friends.

Eleven-year-old Devon excelled at math and science in school but was socially isolated. Devon's family and Shahla saw that his interest in video games could be a bridge to his relationship with other children. A virtual basketball game that Devon enjoyed offered the opportunity to play cooperatively with others. At first, Shahla and the research team showed Devon's father how to play in ways that encouraged Devon to initiate social interactions around the game, such as asking to split screens, share controllers, and even pass the ball. Devon's father then encouraged some cousins to play the cooperative version. In time, Devon and his cousins found common ground through the game and other virtual basketball and baseball games. The family often tapped Devon's deep knowledge of baseball and basketball statistics to enhance everyone's enjoyment of the games.

We can be on the lookout for interactions, large and small, that take advantage of the power of reciprocity to build our child's world. Our child's ability to move through these moments brings its own kind of mastery. That's one reason that therapists work hard to teach very young children with autism how to imitate other people. Once our child can imitate others in different ways and situations, they are better equipped to learn many more things and faster. Their ability to learn and master new things can become so powerful that some structured teaching becomes obsolete for them, and reciprocity fills the gap. Reciprocity gives us access to new relationships. It's like the difference for all of us after we learn to read—then we read to learn. We enjoy reading, too. We access new worlds when we read.

These big moments don't stop in childhood. In their paper on behavioral cusps and person-centered interventions, Garnett Smith and colleagues described Sarah, who was twenty-two. Sarah's grandparents were concerned that she was a homebody. She enjoyed watching college basketball on television. Her grandparents took a chance and encouraged a friend to take Sarah to a game. She enjoyed herself so much that she continued attending games and other large events. Her reciprocal interactions with other people increased exponentially. She talked with workers at the concession stand and with the players after the game. She participated in halftime activities. Her world expanded. In fact, Sarah developed a whole new set of social skills around the experience, a classic example of a behavioral cusp. She was much less of a homebody. She even asked her grandparents to go to other sporting events.

We can be on the lookout, then, for activities that capture reciprocal contingencies. Our child can join other family members preparing the table for a meal. They can take turns playing a board game with a sibling. They can write thank-you notes. In this way, everyone can be our child's ally. Life is filled with many gentle back-and-forth interactions, all worth fostering because they make life better and have the potential to create their own sustaining energy for our child's progress.

For example, Sam couldn't tolerate haircuts when he was a toddler. Peggy resorted to cutting his hair while he slept. It worked well enough, but when her next-door neighbor, Judy, a stylist, heard how they were coping, she offered to help. Judy brought her supplies to the house. Sam sat in the high chair in front of a full-length mirror in the living room. Sam told Judy how to hold his hair as she cut it. She was patient and went along with his directions, and still managed to cut it well.

When the family moved, Peggy wondered whether she would have to find someone willing to make house calls, like Judy did. She found another stylist. Connie had a big heart and boundless sense of humor. She kept Sam looking good from boyhood trims through the high school trends.

The whole family got their haircuts on the same day. Connie would ask Sam who was next in the chair and everyone conferred on the plans. As he got older, Sam stopped telling Connie how to hold his hair and let her cut it as she would for any client. Then, the conversation became whatever Sam or Connie wanted to talk about. Getting haircuts became a powerful lesson in reciprocity. Judy opened the door, and Connie showed how reciprocity builds those connections. She understood that the circle of what is given and received grows wider with the years.

Then Connie got cancer. Sam understood that she became too weak to stand all day and cut people's hair. He found another barber. The relationships, begun by the simple act of cutting Sam's hair, had brought out the best in everyone. When Connie died a year later, Sam and the rest of the family felt the loss of a friend. They still miss her.

Building Strength and Resilience

Being deeply loved by someone gives you strength, while loving someone deeply gives you courage.
- Lao Tzu

☙

We may look to others to lend us strength when we face a challenge or try to meet a goal. But other people can also help us build our own strength and resilience. One family that Shahla knew hired a new speech therapist to work with their son, who had a speech impediment. Oscar's previous speech therapist was sweet and likeable. He really enjoyed the time he spent with her. Yet, Oscar had made little progress in the year he had already spent in therapy.

Alia, the new therapist, re-evaluated Oscar's skills and started a new approach. For the summer they worked together, Alia designed a rigorous, remedial speech and language intervention for Oscar that involved a lot of movement and fun. She tweaked the steps as she implemented the program along the way. Oscar's mother arrived at the end of a session one day that summer to find both Oscar and Alia sweaty and smiling. "We found it!" they both shouted, beaming. "It" was the sound "th."

Like a captain, Alia also worked with Oscar on his reading lessons. Oscar, his family, and Alia worked hard that summer. They had a grueling routine of morning sessions twice a week. Alia gave the family a notebook full of things to do—serious stuff that required adjustment, effort, and time. The homework didn't always get done. Oscar didn't always enjoy it.

Oscar's mother began to see how uncomfortable she was when her son struggled. Alia seemed to expect intense effort and said little about that struggle to the family, but she was a vanguard in sharing a valuable lesson about discomfort: children must work hard, and they will become strong by learning to carry their own crosses. That summer, Oscar's mother learned how to step back and let her son grow stronger.

Years of intensive, deliberate, purposeful, and fast work in Sam's early childhood made him vulnerable to helplessness. The way everyone worked with him required his compliance in learning the skills that are part of growing up. At the same time, his parents, teachers, and therapists remained mindful of his agency. Many issues in raising a young child with autism read like a how-to checklist: how to feed oneself, how to dress, how to toilet train, how to get out the door in the morning. Yet, there are other, more complicated things our child and family must master that don't fit the how-to formula as they grow up, such as fostering relationships, speaking one's truth, and resilience. Without an awareness of the interplay between a child's compliance and agency, we may inadvertently create helplessness and a lack of resilience.

The principal assigned a new teacher's aide to Sam in middle school. The aide packed his backpack between classes for several weeks before a teacher noticed and set things right. For several years prior, Sam had packed up for himself between classes. However, because of many years working to gain his cooperation in general, he said nothing when his new aide took over.

Most children have a little spark in them that fosters their independence, strength, and resilience. We might call it obstinance when we're seeking a little more cooperation. The situations in which a child with autism appears to have the least flexibility is sometimes the place to foster their strength and resilience.

Shahla worked with one preschooler who had a few routines that he loved. At home, he lined up empty plastic bottles and started his routine by taking a small sniff from one bottle (his mother made sure they were clean), and then he danced and flipped around them. At school, he had a routine with giant Tinker toys. That routine grew quite elaborate and took about twenty minutes to complete. The young boy's team, led by graduate student Jessica Potucek, recognized that his preference showed he was capable of long, complex, and interesting behavioral chains. They made the most of that capability and worked with him to expand his routines in ways that were flexible and more likely to put him in contact with other people and activities. They began in a way that was similar to Yummy Starts: they systematically introduced new actions related to those he enjoyed. They gave him choices to add similar responses before completing the actions he already loved. By changing the contingencies, they worked with him to expand his world and build resilience.

Another preschooler, Darius, brought his favorite stuffed animal to the clinic. The little stuffed pig was probably cute at one time, but by the time Darius was bringing the pig to the clinic, it looked like a prop from a horror film. Darius's other favorite play came from rolls of colored masking tape. He taped the seams to keep the stuffing from coming out of his Franken-Pig. Some of the colored tape was faded; some of it was dirty. But Shahla and the team didn't force Darius to give up his friend. They devised several ways to expand his interactions, using Franken-Pig. They dressed Franken-Pig in ways that made it look a little less horrible to the rest of the world. They incorporated Franken-Pig into his other play. Over time, Darius agreed to let go of Franken-Pig for short periods so the toy could sit on a shelf and "watch" Darius play, a key step toward building his resilience.

Peggy gained her own insight into encouraging Sam's resilience from a family tradition of going bowling on Christmas Day. When the younger children were learning to bowl, they would hit pins, but they would also throw a lot of gutter balls. Then, the bowling alley offered lanes with bumper guards. The bumpers helped the kids hit more pins, and eliminated the occasional gutter ball. The bumper lanes set young bowlers up for success. The grown-ups sat back after they saw that bumper guards helped the kids better learn to bowl on their own, learning faster to throw better. As the children got older, they were ready to leave the bumper lanes and bowl in a lane with the grown-ups.

We should not stand over kids, including children with autism, to help them throw all the balls. That's not how to make a strong and resilient kid. With each situation, each problem, each opportunity for growth, we need to think about where to install those metaphorical bumper guards, then stand back and let the kids throw. All children, including our child with autism, need the adults in their lives to stand at the periphery. We need to stay far enough back that the kids see that they are doing things on their own, yet an adult is nearby in case of trouble. When we act as a bumper guard, then, we reinforce resilience as the kids get stronger. Kids know they don't have to worry about hitting a lot of pins just yet—they are still going to throw gutter balls. But they will be happy to just keep throwing because they are doing it on their own. They will get stronger and throw straighter balls. Soon, they'll be ready to go without the bumpers. Even after that, they know they will hit some spares and strikes and some gutters. And that's okay.

When behavior analysts design the supports for change, they can arrange the stimulus controls—the bumper guards—to prompt, constrain, or deflect ways of responding that encourage our children to develop their own strength in particular situations. They continue altering those supports until our child achieves the desired independence.

How each of us sees independence and dependence can vary within a family, a community, and a culture. While making treatment plans and decisions, both parents and professionals should take the time to understand the family values and what makes a happy life. A child may need to learn good sleep habits, but he may not need to learn those habits sleeping alone if his family sleeps all in one room.

The science behind any treatment plan won't be compromised when professionals respect our family's values and our culture. Behavior analysts and other helping professions continue to make their own practices stronger and more resilient by learning to listen and respond to people who have different backgrounds and life experiences from their own. This includes the family's perspectives and value systems and the child's emerging perspectives and opinions about the course of their life. Moreover, our children will do things, learn things, seek things that make us uncomfortable. We have to let them. They are becoming their own. If we don't let them, they won't be resilient enough to survive.

Learning From Each Other

The real voyage of discovery consists not in seeking new landscapes, but in having new eyes.
- Marcel Proust

Shahla worked with one family whose child, Elijah, had a dual diagnosis of Down syndrome and autism. The double-barreled condition isolated the family a little, especially when they watched other families draw strength from the way their babies with Down syndrome expressed love and attachment. That wasn't happening for Elijah's family. His dual diagnosis also complicated relationships with teachers and therapists. More things could go wrong for both parents and professionals, such as slipping into resignation (a hazardous attitude) over Elijah's apparent lack of attachment to caregivers.

Instead, Elijah's mother spent hours reading about Down syndrome at the library and online. When she found the information she was seeking, she brought it to Shahla. The critical information explained how certain difficulties inherent to Down syndrome (such as the motor delays that kept Elijah from lifting his head to watch his parents and find toys) interacted with the social difficulties in autism (such as Elijah's restricted interests and limited requests of the people around him). Shahla recognized that Elijah's mother had uncovered information the team needed to work with Elijah to make progress. Together, Shahla's team and Elijah's mother also learned enough so that her baby boy learned to smile.

We feel good when we smile, and it makes other people feel good, too. When we are teaching, our child's smile tells us something else important: that we've found a sweet spot in their learning. Program goals, stimulus control, and a well-timed reinforcing event all meet at such sweet spots. Our child's smile also signals their feelings and tells us about the conditions that help them make progress. Elijah's smile meant the team had found a sweet spot.

Shahla and Elijah's mother designed a program based on what the latter had unearthed about motor difficulties in Down syndrome and what Shahla knew about reinforcement in autism interventions. Together, they built a therapy sequence that taught Elijah to look toward others and engage with them socially. They experimented to find toys he would reach for. He liked a vibrating, musical light wand enough to use his muscles in new ways. Eventually, he lifted his head to look into people's eyes and see them smiling at him. As he progressed, he smiled back.

Parents can join professionals in building a community of practice around their child. Each person will have different experiences, vantage points, and ways to approach shared goals. We share a mission in the commitment to help our child and to always improve in how we do that work. To practice well, we work with intention, reflecting on what we learned, what worked, and what didn't work. We recalibrate our practice when necessary to stay in the desired direction.

Sometimes parents can face obstacles as they try to work in partnership with professionals. Because parents often rely on experts, they can have a harder time working with and questioning authority in such groups, whether formal or informal. However, parents should let professionals know their goals and when the work doesn't suit those goals. Sometimes we can explain and shift a professional's perspective. Sometimes the professional shifts our perspective. Other times, as Peggy learned when Sam had trouble at the dentist, we might decide to find someone new.

When Sam was a toddler, he began seeing the dentist. He learned to cooperate before he got too old or learned to be fearful. He sat for exams, x-rays, and cleanings. When he was twelve years old, the roots of his last set of baby teeth didn't dissolve underneath the permanent teeth. The baby teeth got stuck. The dentist referred Sam to another dentist who could sedate him for a safe extraction.

Sam didn't tolerate the anesthesia well, but he recovered. Peggy saw that Sam was ready to return to regular checkups, but the new dentist had other ideas. He had Sam come back every three months to sit in the chair, but he didn't clean Sam's teeth or take x-rays. He told Peggy he was rebuilding trust. After a year of these trust-building visits, the new dentist said it was time to make an appointment to sedate Sam for a cleaning and exam.

Peggy tried to talk to him, but he didn't appear to give much weight to Sam's many years of cooperation with other dentists. Peggy sensed something wasn't right, but she couldn't put her finger on it just then. She needed more time to think. She left the dentist's office with the pledge to call and make an appointment. But she never did. Peggy and the dentist could have had a deeper discussion about his proposed change to the practice in Sam's dental care. For example, they needed to answer a key question about whether this new practice could set up a lifelong pattern for Sam: would he be exposed to higher-risk procedures than was necessary?

Instead, Peggy called her own dentist and asked him to treat Sam. He was reluctant. He knew the other dentist had a good reputation for treating difficult cases. Young patients with disabilities can be unpredictable, a risky prospect for a dentist with sharp instruments in tiny places. Peggy was more forthcoming with her own dentist while talking about her goals for Sam, in part because she felt she had little to lose but also because she knew his wife had worked with children with disabilities. Peggy suggested that he could treat Sam as any other anxious patient because he had been cooperating for years. She held her breath. He agreed.

Sam started with an appointment for a cleaning with a dental hygienist. The hygienist scheduled extra time and took many breaks as she worked. Sam asked many questions and the hygienist answered them. She took the suggestion to try an ultrasonic tool at first, a suggestion that came from Peggy's father, a dentist who treated patients from a group home before he retired. As the years went by, Sam learned to tolerate the scraper and the probe. He cooperated as the dentist put sealants on his molars. When he turned eighteen years old and it was time for his wisdom teeth to come out, he came through the anesthesia just fine.

Her father, her own dentist, and the hygienists all lent their professional reasoning so that Sam could visit the dentist without sedation and without fear. He's never had a cavity.

Seeing Around Our Blind Spots

I asked the French artist Henri Matisse whether, when eating a tomato, he looked at it the way an artist would. "No," he said. "When I eat a tomato, I look at it the way anyone else would. But when I paint a tomato, then I see it differently."
- Gertrude Stein
☙

By collaborating, we can help each other see different perspectives, dangers, options, and possibilities. We can also learn to see around our hazardous attitudes and limitations.

While waiting for a special education team meeting, a mother named Lexi admitted to Shahla that she didn't understand her own blind spots in decision-making until she had a child with a disability. Lexi's son was six. Both women anticipated a contentious meeting. Shahla watched Lexi gaze out the window. Then, Lexi turned to Shahla and told her about a time before she was married, when she had worked as a school administrator. She had blocked another mother's efforts to set new goals for her child during a team meeting.

"His mother wanted him to learn to administer his own breathing treatments," she told Shahla. "I was adamant that he absolutely could not do this. No matter how many meetings we had, I wouldn't bend. It was against the rules and I just didn't think it was safe." She paused for a long time, then added, "I just didn't understand."

For the mother of the boy who needed to learn to administer his own breathing treatments, Lexi was a barrier. Back then, she didn't see the value in figuring out alternative ways to work with the rules so that he could learn to care for himself and become more independent.

During that long wait with Shahla, Lexi re-evaluated what it meant to have someone who cared for her son's long-term well-being. Sometimes planning and decision-making can trigger odd dynamics in a group of people. An individual team member may be blinded to the big picture for a little while as they focus on the issue in front of them. While working in groups, we sometimes forget that when we win an argument, someone we care about loses that argument—and that ultimately means we lose, too. Our shared purposes work like a giant orchestration: each person brings their training and talents to the team; together, the sound becomes something else altogether, something creative, new, moving, and powerful.

Blind spots can happen with the best intentions. An example of that recently emerged when one behavior analyst saw the possibilities of working with many families by setting up an autism treatment center. The center was so successful that a large company operating in many states bought the business. Insurance helped pay for the services, and many families came to the center because it was well run and the children made progress.

After the merger, the company continued expanding to meet demand for services for the growing number of children being diagnosed. There were rumblings of trouble. One family reported that their son had started talking but stopped after going to one of the new centers. In addition, the boy, who was content to be inactive before (perhaps almost *too* content to be inactive), had grown aggressive and stopped responding to his parents.

A new graduate got a job at the center. She complained that she saw her supervisor in group once a month—enough time only to sign off on programs, and no more. She also expressed concerns about several incidents that seemed wrong. For example, after one child's outburst, therapists told a family they had to cancel plans for a family trip to a theme park, a devastating blow to the child and the siblings, who had looked forward to the event for months.

The lead behavior analyst had focused on expanding the business to serve many more children. Meanwhile, treatment had withered from lack of assessment, master skills, and attention. The center grew and met the demand, but the staff themselves weren't connecting to children and families as they needed. The children's progress often plateaued or regressed. The team's desire to meet demand caused a blind spot.

Parents can have blind spots, too. One mother came to researchers John Lutzker and Randy Campbell for help with her daughter, Ann. The young girl required regular doctor visits and was now vomiting in the car on the way to the medical offices. Her mother reported that Ann's fear had become so pervasive that she gagged at associations, such as seeing blood on television. The team started with assessments and talking with the mother. They watched how she prepared for doctor trips, which involved steps she didn't take for other car trips. She lined the car with sheets. She wrapped Ann in a sheet. On the way, she asked Ann how she was feeling and even stopped the car if it appeared that Ann was going to get upset. Inadvertently, the mother may have established the conditions for Ann to vomit.

At one point during their work together, Ann had to be taken for medical care after an accident. Ann's mother didn't prepare for the trip, and Ann did not vomit. This gave the team further information to develop an approach that would alleviate everyone's discomfort. At first, Ann's mother didn't understand the plan. The plan still involved preparation: both Ann and her mom practiced going to the physician without the sheets and, instead, playing with Ann's preferred toys. The sheets that had served as a cue for distress and vomiting were taken away. On the next trip to the doctor, Ann's mother didn't prepare for trouble and spent the trip laughing and playing.

Of course, we can identify with Ann's mother and that basic desire to protect everyone from a car full of vomit. The desire to protect our children and ourselves creates blind spots. Ann's mother knew her daughter was in trouble, but she needed other perspectives to see her role in alleviating her daughter's fears. We can also see how Lexi created a professional blind spot from the basic desire to do her job correctly as a young school administrator. Lexi was responsible for making sure that children received their needed medication while at school. Had a student missed their medication and become ill, she would have been devastated and may have faced disciplinary action.

While most professionals know that trying to help everyone could result in helping no one, they can develop blind spots, too. Most of the time, we can help each other see around our blind spots, especially when we understand that basic desire to respond to children in distress. But in the case of the systemic blind spots at the troubled treatment center, the change had to be systemic, too. Parents can't always wait for systems to change. Some parents just left the center and sought services elsewhere. That is a reasonable response when parents have that choice. Parents of children with disabilities are already hoeing an uphill road. They aren't required to spend their time and energy on institutions and systems that aren't dealing with their own blind spots.

Being an Equal Among Professionals

Are not five sparrows sold for two small coins? Yet not one of them has escaped the notice of God. Even the hairs of your head have been counted. Do not be afraid. You are worth more than many sparrows.
- Luke 12:6-7

Parents may find themselves deferring to professionals regarding decisions about their child's care, but we cannot be afraid of the people who have control over the direction our child's life might take. A parent's wisdom together with a professional's expertise can boost a child's progress in powerful ways. Parents may sometimes need to assert what they know about their child. Topping the list for important times to do so: special education planning meetings and clinic informed-consent discussions.

When Sam was in kindergarten, Peggy thought he could benefit from occupational therapy. She found a professor with a clinical practice at Texas Woman's University, and the elementary school contracted for their services.

Sam went once a week for fifty minutes when school was in session. The sessions also provided practical experience for a pair of students assigned to work with the professor in the clinic each semester. Held after school and supervised full time by the professor, the sessions cost the school district a nominal amount. Sam made significant progress with his physical development, motor planning, and more during the sessions.

After two years, something broke down between the special education director and the university professor. The special education director decided to end the service contract. Peggy sensed that both sides had good reasons for the conflict, but neither told her what they were.

The special education director arranged for Sam and several other students served by the contract to meet with another occupational therapist. The sessions were in another city. The new contract cost the school four times as much. The therapist was top-notch, and her clients made good progress. Peggy could see that the special education director worked hard to find the best solution. Sam would also have to learn to interact with a new person and a new routine, which can be a healthy challenge. But the school had just gone through several staffing changes with speech therapists, and that alone had cost Sam months of progress.

Peggy and Mark also knew something about Sam that others tended to forget. Sam was motivated to talk, but he was, and remains to this day, defensive to being touched. Sam would need months to trust a new occupational therapist and begin making progress again.

Moreover, Mark's work schedule was too erratic for him to drive Sam twenty miles each week to the new clinic. Peggy couldn't shuttle Sam to the appointments without compromising her work schedule, either. If the school bussed Sam to the appointments, the teachers expected that travel time to cut into his regular class time.

Without knowing more about the reasons for the change, Peggy and Mark refused the offer with the new therapist and insisted that the contract with the university be renewed. The school superintendent stepped in.

He called a meeting with the special education director. Peggy and Mark were nervous. Would they be confronted with new information that would diminish the family's concerns? The special education director gave no additional reasons for the change. After the superintendent listened to both the director and to Peggy and Mark, he decided the family's reasoning was sound. He asked the director to renew the contract with the university clinic.

The sessions continued for several more years, and Sam flourished. He stayed in touch with the professor even after she retired and moved to another state. Perhaps the outcome would have been different had the special education director chose to share her reasons. But the situation shows that parents bring important values, information, and perspective to treatment decisions, especially when those decisions have implications for the long term.

Like many parents, Peggy and Mark didn't always feel prepared for special education planning meetings. The annual reviews were stressful because the two of them were often expected to hear Sam's test results and make decisions about them in the same meeting, sometimes without much explanation of what information the evaluation had sought and what the diagnosticians had found. In their first special education team meeting, a speech therapist announced to the team her results, noting that Sam, then three years old, did not point to his nose when asked. Peggy asked the group what that meant. The speech therapist, who was fresh out of school, couldn't answer the question. No one else did, either.

The speech therapist later showed the family great deference. She called a few days after the meeting. She was bothered that she couldn't explain why it was important that Sam didn't touch his nose when asked. She conferred with her former professor. She explained to Peggy that Sam wasn't imitating the speech therapist during the evaluation, an important skill in learning to talk. She made sure the family understood what they needed to do in working with their son as he learned how to learn. Her deference to them in answering that question proved a watershed moment in his progress.

Researchers have found that many parents of children with autism say that getting services is among the most stressful jobs in raising their child. Some parents feel they have to fight for explanations and services. Other parents feel even more stress because they know that school officials consider them difficult.

Parents' perceptions of how they are viewed may often be well founded. Peggy's mother began a second career as a special education aide after Sam's diagnosis. Because she was willing to change diapers and work with children on other challenging tasks, she was assigned to some of the most difficult cases and found camaraderie with teachers who shared a mission to make a difference. However, during her lunch hours in the teacher's break room, she was surprised to occasionally hear other staff members describe parents in uncharitable terms, criticizing families for their values and decisions. Yet, we know that poor communication between grown-ups can impact a child's progress. Not surprisingly, researchers have found that poor communication is a contributing factor in litigation between parents and schools.

We parents can feel better prepared for meetings, or any occasion that we need to talk with teachers, therapists, or administrators, by planning ahead and practicing what we want to say. We might even seek a bit of coaching to boost our effectiveness.

Showing deference to one another can make a difference. Professionals should not think of parents as difficult or just another barrier to work around. A professional doesn't have to share a family's values in order to offer their skills while respecting and deferring to those values. Nor can parents think of professionals as hardliners or eggheads lacking common sense or compassion. As a general rule, professional reasoning does not focus solely on what's happening in the clinic at the moment. Professionals can also see a long-term course of action that supports our child's future. They have an ethical responsibility to be our child's ally. Even when we disagree, we parents can find a way to incorporate professional reasoning in our decision-making so that expertise shines through our planning and programs.

By showing deference to each other, we are better equipped to make observations and decisions for our child that can go from small to large. We start by observing what is happening with our child, including all the small details. We work together to find patterns in those observations and details. We may find that our best observations and projections come from knowing what happened before, both the past events and the details that lead up to them. We can make some projections by using our keenest observations. Professionals bring their knowledge of similar patterns reported in the research. Sorting through all that solid evidence and sound reasoning, we decide which actions we can take that offer the best chance of making progress.

We must also defer to what our child says or shows is important to them. That needs to be part of all our long-term goals. As a high schooler, Sam participated in his special education team meetings when it was time to plan his transition to work life and higher education. He received additional training on self-advocacy as an adult, relearning the lessons of deference even for himself.

Several years ago, Sam was in line to board an airplane when the crew announced that they had to do another bag search at the gate. Sam was caught off guard, as many other travelers were. He wasn't able to repack his bag as quickly as the other travelers. Some of them got impatient with him. That unnerved him even more and made it harder still for him to adjust. A gate attendant stepped in to help him. Peggy asked him whether that might have been a good time to disclose his autism—not to the impatient people around him but to the gate attendant who was helping him. Peggy suggested that his disclosure to the gate attendant may have been overheard by some fellow travelers nearby and triggered a bit of deference toward him, unless they were real jerks. Most people are good and want to be kind to others, she told him, so those fellow travelers might have been embarrassed at their impatience and inability to be kinder and more observant. But Sam disagreed that it would have been a good idea to disclose, and that was his prerogative. It's not his job to help the world not be a jerk.

In all the activity around a child with autism, we could be tempted to hand off some responsibility. The job can feel like big rocks in our everyday lives. But when we are like water, we can move the rocks. There is cumulative power in combining a trained professional's expertise and rational intelligence with the experience and emotional and spiritual intelligence that a parent, and the individual with autism, brings to the decision-making.

We must try not to fear one another. Instead, we listen and defer to one another. When we do that, we are deferring to hope.

Sharing Wisdom and Responsibility

Your intuition and parental instincts are good and reliable. You will lose nothing by changing your mind about priorities. You have no obligation to live with guilt. You know your child best. Your child needs you just because you are you.
- Randall Colton Rolfe

⁓

When our child receives an autism diagnosis, and perhaps even before it becomes official, the work required of us makes our lives busy. We search for the right toys, the best treatment plan, the most reputable teachers, therapists, and doctors. Resources matter, but ready access to resources doesn't mean we can buy a better life. We make our life better with wisdom, intention, and community.

So even if resources are scarce, we can still do a lot. It will take many incremental steps and many repetitions of those steps to coax our child to meet our eyes, to imitate us as we raise our arms to the sky, to speak those first words. We read books and articles. We ask people for help, including other, more experienced parents. We need the latest and best that science has to offer our child and our family. We become aware that we will be a kind of science consumer for the rest of our lives.

The first discoveries in autism treatment became the foundation for new scientific discoveries that continue to inform both research and clinical treatment. Applied behavior analysts laid the original groundwork with deliberation and care. They used science to build their knowledge and techniques, and for most of them, love was their bridge—an arc bending toward sound principles and justice. Their purposeful actions proved key to their success.

Treatment is hard work. Treatment can also be intrusive, arbitrary, and exhausting—particularly for families at their most fragile point—when professionals skim over the purpose of their actions. Even the most dedicated professional will shift their focus toward making payroll, keeping the lights on, and eking out a profit from time to time. When they do, treatment conditions can change. That change can be slight or seismic, since each action we take declares our intentions. Our child needs more than skilled and respectful service from professionals. To make progress, our child needs wise, purposeful, intentional actors in their life.

A wise therapist will challenge themselves to come up with myriad ways to teach a child in their natural environment and to make progress. The beauty of their effort and humanity comes without a price tag. We can't deny that families with ample resources may have an easier time finding the help they need. Some families live where skilled therapists and other good help abound. Other families are isolated, by culture or location, and must work harder in other ways to gather resources they need. Priorities in our public policy can make it easier or harder to access resources. Money, or the lack of it, can affect what happens and what is possible for a child with autism and their family, depending on how the money flows.

Still, no one wants the commodification of autism services to get in the way of being loving and doing the right thing. Parents and professionals can guard against this interference by asking these simple questions: What are we buying and why? What are they selling and why? A truthful answer isn't complicated. We buy and sell goods and services all the time. Commodification is part of our culture. Buying and selling doesn't inherently put love and souls in jeopardy.

For example, when Sam was a preschooler, Peggy took him to a beautiful toy store two or three times a month. The store stocked toys that offered rich play experiences. Children, along with the grown-ups, were welcome to explore the shelves. By that point in the family's life, a speech therapist from the county office of education visited once a week and showed the family how to use toys to foster Sam's speech and social development. Peggy tried to invest in toys that Sam responded to best, but sometimes she picked out toys that she found charming or triggered a sense of longing. Because the family's resources were limited, she learned from those mistakes. The family also borrowed toys from a toy library, which made picking out the wrong toy less costly.

By contrast, Shahla worked with one well-to-do family who had a daughter with autism. Shahla noticed that the girl's mother also bought many toys: cause-and-effect toys, wind-up toys, construction toys. The family could afford all the toys their daughter would ever need, and the toys available for her happiness and treatment could outfit a toy library five times over.

Both families' experiences show that money acted as a simple tool of exchange. Their children made progress through the purposeful, intentional use of those toys, not because the families acquired toys. No toy will fix a child. Neither family could buy skills or relief from anxiety and stress, no matter how much or how little money they had. In fact, the act of acquiring things can trigger its own stress when it becomes wasteful. Then again, when the time comes to decide where our limited resources will go for our child, we do them no favors by saying "why bother?"

Today, more autism services are funded by all of us, a responsibility we share through public schools and health care systems. Every child has a better chance today because several generations of parents and advocates pressed for change in those systems. Schools, insurers, and autism service providers declare their intentions with their funding decisions, so we need to ask questions and understand the answers and their implications. Which treatment will be funded? What will it accomplish? When and how will it end?

Even with established protocols, families (and their insurers, for that matter) aren't guaranteed sophisticated services. In treatment centers, children may spend much of their time with behavior techs who have minimal training and supervision. In other words, we may be getting excellent child care instead of appropriate, effective treatment. Or worse, sometimes the care isn't even good child care. The same can happen in schools when children spend the day in an isolated room with a well-meaning but poorly equipped para-professional. We cannot hand our child over at the front door. We must be good consumers. Otherwise, we risk jeopardizing our child's healthy growth and development, even their attachment to our family. We ask questions and become discerning consumers, understanding the consumer protections and responsibilities that are part of any business.

No matter what goes wrong, families don't have to suffer when professional intentions and actions get off track. We need only tap the strength we've had all along—the determination and love we have for our child and each other—to keep progress on the right path. When both parents and professionals remain focused on the intentions of their actions, we can minimize harm and increase everyone's resilience.

We can also seek wisdom from parents and professionals who've gone before us. Parents of autistic children often help one another with networks and tips about nearby resources. We feel a kinship, much like new parents who get together to share information on everything from who understands how to get the baby to sleep through the night, to finding a pediatrician.

We know that sharing our hard-won wisdom can lighten another parent's burden. For example, some parents like to share Emily Perl Kingsley's essay, "Welcome to Holland," because its hopeful tone can help families who are new to a diagnosis, even if the essay doesn't begin to tackle all the issues a family can expect to face. Kingsley's son was born with Down syndrome, and her essay uses a travel metaphor of an unexpected stop in another country to explain that although parenting a child with a disability may not fulfill one's expectations, it's no less beautiful than parenting a child without a disability.

Finding others who've shared at least some of our experiences can help us maintain a sense of humor—that higher perspective that keeps bitterness at bay and friendships close by. Good friends will invite us to dinner, and the best ones will also rejoice and laugh with us when our kid announces in the middle of a dinner party that they have to poop.

Shared wisdom also helps us avoid the charlatans. They seem to be everywhere, ready to take advantage of families that are in need or afraid, even families who have only a little bit of money to spend. Some offer bogus treatment. Others will string families along, charging top dollar long after the value is gone.

In this way, parents build communities for their families. This community-building work can become more powerful when done with intention. For example, we might join a babies group for the conversation, a preschool group for playdates, or a sports group for help with building skills. Community groups often center around what's happening with the children and the community's degree of passion for the activity and for one another. These communities will shift and change as our child grows. Before the internet, individuals who were physically different from the community around them often had a harder time finding kindred spirits and support. A babies group may not be a source of much shared wisdom, for example, when our challenges are different from those of the other infants whose growth and development follow a more typical path. But when we search with discernment, the internet has made finding and creating these intentional communities a little easier for us.

All these ways that we share the burden of responsibility—finding people and resources, building communities—need advocacy to grow and flourish. We may find ourselves gravitating to other parent warriors as we wage the next generation of public policy battles or private battles for our child's treatment and services. When we are in a battle, we need alliances. But we also need a healthy perspective. We can triage and decide the most urgent places to put our attention and resources. Life with autism, by the way, is not an unending battle. If we find ourselves locking horns a lot with the people around us, we may need to stop and take stock. We can either make sure the battle we are fighting isn't coming from within or figure out how to get out of a very bad environment.

We will meet with many professionals over the years, particularly when we enter the health care system and after our children start school. Advocacy groups offer assistance, including representatives, to attend meetings with us. They also offer training, which is worthwhile for most parents. Advocacy is both a learned skill and a balancing act.

In her graduate research, Heather Barahona asked parents and caregivers whether they felt intimidated and ineffective during meetings with school professionals. Most parents reported having those feelings. Parents also felt overwhelmed by the new vocabulary and the meeting protocols that have evolved from laws governing special education. With Shahla as her faculty advisor, Barahona studied training tools and taught parents ways to communicate during meetings. Some of that training included role-playing and giving parents feedback on their attempts. Her training also included scripts that included the kinds of questions most parents or caregivers need to ask. The training helped caregivers know when to speak up as well as the statements they may need to make. After the training, parents and caregivers reported feeling better equipped to advocate for their child, especially in team planning meetings.

A tiny but mighty tool emerged from Barahona's research: a bookmark, a small job aid that parents can use when advocating for their children with disabilities. As both the parent of a child with a disability and as a teacher, Barahona understood more than one perspective as she learned to advocate for her daughter. She knew what it was like to be both the professional and the parent on the team, particularly that lone parent up against a roomful of professionals trying not to give the student too much.

Accordingly, the front of the bookmark listed things for parents to ask about, or keep in mind, during the planning meetings. That sent a signal to the rest of the team: this list is so important that the parent made it into a job aid to help them do their best in the meeting. The back of the bookmark had a photo of each child. The photo reminded early intervention teams how important this tender child was to their discussion. The gesture could make a parent somewhat vulnerable to the rest of the team, but Barahona also knew that the teachers, therapists, and administrators loved children. Some team members had children of their own who were the center of their worlds. The bookmark was openly shared, picture and list, at the beginning of the meeting.

The bookmark technique proved smart and effective. We know that most adults have better discussions and make better decisions if they understand why something is important. The bookmark became an indicator of a shared reinforcer, reminding everyone on the team why the meeting was happening, while acknowledging and setting expectations for it. The bookmark cued respect for the team's work in how they selected and measured goals for Barahona's daughter and other children.

The bookmark reminds us of the power of shared reinforcers, about being prepared, and working with others on our team. It also reminds us that it's good to be explicit about what is happening and to bring our truthful, authentic self to the discussion. We bring the power of our humanity to the meeting, telling everyone that this is how we want it to be and, with that, allowing everyone to bring their full humanity as we all move to the next step.

Parents should consider that value before growing too dependent on others to do all the advocacy for their families. It's okay to get help. There may even be times that we don't realize we need help as we are receiving it. But even with those times, we can guard against our own learned helplessness. An advocate might work with us to get past a particular barrier, but they cannot possibly know all that is important to us and our child. That's our job.

In the Family

And I will not change the last word of the story. It is still love.
- Clara Claiborne Park

    Parenting brings much joy. We also have sorrow, particularly when we see how our own shortcomings and shortfalls affect the entire family. Parenting roles are different over time, cultures, and circumstances. Still, adulthood brings new boundaries and roles. Even for adults with profound autism and other disabilities, everything changes in adulthood. The big discussions about how much responsibility parents have in that individual's life—or how much siblings have after parents die—can get complicated. Many of us tend to avoid talking about that responsibility we have to one another. Where are the dividing lines among society and a father, mother, a brother or sister and a person with a disability? For all of us, the responsibility for our own daily actions is clear. But the oldest moral dilemma remains: how am I my brother's keeper?

    While we wrestle with those questions, we must consider how our entire family is learning, connecting, and loving. Families that have the skills they need, both large and small, are more resilient. These skills are built over time among parents, siblings, and in some cultures, extended family and friends. It works best when the information and connections start early and include every family member.

    In their classic 1994 text on family ecology, applied behavior analysts John Lutzker and Randy Campbell describe a family that is a composite of the many families they worked with over the years. In this composite family, the second child, Sean, has a severe disability. He speaks very little and is growing increasingly aggressive. The older sister is acting out. The mother has quit her job to care for the children full time. Both parents are stressed about money, and their relationship has deteriorated. The father is resorting to corporal punishment more often. His default response in spanking Sean has compromised trust within the family. The family has also become more insular, limiting their contact with the outside world.

    In working with this family, Lutzker and Campbell could have set up a treatment plan designed to reduce Sean's aggression. However, they saw the obligation to do more than that. They worked with the whole family as a system, addressing things such as planning successful, enjoyable family time at home, as well as relaxation and parenting techniques. They also focused on increasing Sean's skills. As Sean began to better express his wants and needs rather than melting down in frustration, his behavior changed. Wisdom lay in working with Sean on how to communicate, not just how to speak. With those changes, conditions improved for him and for the entire family.

In cases such as this, we might work with our child to point to pictures on a communication board first. As a set of motor skills, pointing can be easier to muster than speaking. This way, our child can tell us when they are hurt, hungry, or need help with something. Therapists can include parents and siblings in such communication programs. The whole family will change how they respond as our child begins to express wants and needs with the picture board. When a child can communicate, they are less likely to act out. When family members learn more ways to interact and engage with their children, conditions for the family change much faster and likely for the better. When family members better respond to one another, parents are less likely to become frustrated and resort to punishment. Siblings are less likely to feel powerless and alone. A wave of change begins, and family members can rebuild and maintain trust in one another. In this way, a family's ecology is like a tidepool, Lutzker and Campbell wrote. A family's ecology can either stagnate or improve with each wave of change.

Not long after Lutzker and Campbell published their work, Shahla befriended a woman whose adult son had autism. Many good people worked with Felix as he grew up, even though information and services were scant at the time. One day, in a quiet moment, the mother told Shahla that the family had not done as well for Felix's brother. They spent so much time and energy on Felix that they dropped the ball while raising his brother. Felix was doing well as an adult, but his brother was in treatment for addiction.

Her hard-earned wisdom reminds us all that when we are in a crisis, it's easy to focus on the child who needs help and overlook the other children. We love all of our children, but some demonstration of that love goes missing when we focus too much or in harmful ways on one part of the family tidepool. For the long haul, we need healthy strategies for the entire family.

Different families will have different values about a sibling's role in treatment. Siblings can be part of the conversations, the planning, and the teaching programs, as much as they are willing and able to be involved. Every family member's well-being and resilience gets a boost when we include the siblings in these discussions.

Researchers continue to examine sibling relationships in order to work with all the children in families with autistic children, so that the family can make progress. Shahla and graduate student Sara Czekalski worked with one family that was similar to the composite family described in Lutzker and Campbell's essay, but this time, the parents decided that the older brother could be a good teacher for his younger sister, who had autism. He wanted to help, too.

The team noticed early in treatment that the little sister often did what her big brother asked but frequently with tears running down her face. The team also saw that the big brother could sometimes be strict. For the sister's sake and for the sake of their relationship, the program needed to change. The family had clear values and expectations about each member's role over time. The team wasn't going to craft different roles for the children. The older sibling would still be the younger sibling's teacher at home. The team retooled the program so that the sister could still make progress and the brother could learn new approaches. The team also made sure to measure the emotions each child displayed so that they documented not only the progress but also the newfound reciprocity and emerging joy in their relationship.

The emotions that siblings display are flags. When we see brothers and sisters hitting each other, crying, or walking away, we might need to stop and regroup until we can understand the contingencies and foster qualities that make for a stronger, lifelong relationship. Behavioral researchers David Celiberti and Sandra Harris recognized this long ago and pioneered ways to help siblings connect. When siblings are smiling, staying close by each other, taking turns, and interacting, they are building a loving relationship for the long term. And parents and professionals have the environment in tune. After all, for most of us, sibling relationships are the longest bonds we have throughout our lives.

The family tidepool is part of a larger social ecosystem. We are shocked when the nightly news reports that a parent has locked their troubled child in a closet or a storage shed. The news triggers a flurry of action, usually by people working in the criminal justice and child welfare systems. Researchers pioneered new ways to respond to child abuse and neglect in the 1970s. These new methods began with a simple piece of wisdom: parents don't set out to abuse their children, but some develop that pattern over time, usually because of missing skills and troubled environments and particularly when the child has a disability.

We've known for decades that families suffer when our social and economic systems are flawed and corrupt. We should not be surprised by what happens to families that are vulnerable and lack resources, as we choke access to community assets and expertise. Without access to information and advocates, whether through the public school and health care systems or in some other way, we reinforce problems for the child with autism and their siblings. We can expect to create more troubled families throughout our community when we are stingy with resources. We must all keep an eye on the tidepools.

Danger Signs and Exit Strategies

Love does not begin and end the way we seem to think it does. Love is a battle, love is a war; love is a growing up.
- James A. Baldwin

Not long after Sam was diagnosed, Mark and Peggy saw a family on a national television talk show that claimed auditory training had helped their daughter with autism. Sam shared the same sensitivities to sound and touch as the girl profiled on the program. Mark and Peggy wondered whether Sam could benefit from the systematic presentation of sounds to learn how to better make sense of them. They looked for an audiologist who could help, and found a practitioner in a nearby city. The audiologist sent them a small packet of information that included some impressive-looking data from recent cases she had treated. Mark and Peggy paid about one-fourth of the audiologist's fee for a full round of treatment and drove more than 100 miles to her office for their first visit.

Sam wouldn't cooperate with the audiologist. She put the earphones on his head. He took them off. She grew frustrated with him. The first session ended soon after it started. The audiologist told Mark and Peggy that Sam would need to learn to tolerate headphones before he could begin treatment.

Mark and Peggy left the office, bewildered. They thought auditory training was a magic bullet for Sam. They thought Sam would listen to sounds and become less sensitive to them as well as to being touched by people or things such as headphones, like the girl on the television show. They had seen that his five senses sometimes bothered him so much that it kept him from learning.

As they made the two-hour drive back home, they took stock of other troubling signs. Unlike the speech therapist who was working with Sam as he learned to talk, the audiologist didn't seem to have the skills to work with Sam. They wondered how much experience she had treating other children with autism. The furniture and fixtures didn't look like the office had been there long. They took a second look at some of the data sheets she provided. The information wasn't scientific, just scientific-looking.

They didn't go back. Instead, they called the audiologist's office, canceled the rest of the sessions, and forfeited the down payment. Sam was upset by the experience, but he wasn't too hurt by it. That made it a little easier for Mark and Peggy to forgive themselves for not having healthy skepticism as they went into an experiment they had learned about on television.

But how can we see the danger signs even among those practitioners who appear to have years of study and science behind their work? Some practitioners will give themselves away by being isolated from the professional community that would hold them accountable. Parents can suss that out by asking a professional how they earned and maintain their credentials as well as by studying the standards of professional societies. For example, behavior analysts who work with clients know and honor the guidelines developed by the Behavior Analysis Certification Board. The Association of Professional Behavior Analysts and Applied Behavior Analysis International support continued learning in the field. Similarly, physicians and other health professions have associations and ethical guidelines, often reinforced through continuing education.

When we know the ethical guidelines for the professionals in our child's life, we will know and should be told when any treatment is off-label or experimental. We want to know, for example, whether a treatment medication about to be prescribed for our child is used primarily for other conditions or has been tested only on adults. We want to know the risks and benefits that the professional will consider as part of the decision and how they will be re-evaluated along the way.

These standards don't mean we should avoid participating in the development of something new. But we should be told what's at stake, and after that, we should give our informed consent to participate. Some patients are eager to be part of a clinical trial, such as a new cancer treatment or vaccine, for example. Researchers outline the risks and benefits before the patients give their informed consent to be a part of such a clinical trial or other research. And before taking that step, researchers put their study's design up for peer review.

Generations ago, doctors experimented on patients without their consent, which triggered major changes in federal laws. Today, any experiment involving a human subject, no matter the research discipline, must be reviewed by experienced peers and vested community members. For most researchers, the institutional review board where they work serves as that body. When the board completes its review and the research design meets the institution's criteria for experimenting on human subjects, the researcher must then fully inform each of the study's participants. The participants must know and understand the benefits and risks of the research before they can give legal consent to the study. Unforeseen risks have emerged during the course of some experiments, at which point scientists and the institutional review boards have a way to shut down the study to protect the people involved.

Other treatment programs aren't scrutinized as closely and formally as research projects, but we can watch for trouble signs just the same. Sometimes trouble emerges when therapists and parents have different motives or conflicting contingencies. We must ask questions of professionals and listen carefully to their answers. That's when the tried-and-true strategies for conflict work best: cool off, ask questions, listen, identify and focus on the issues, find common ground.

Professionals should know and tell us when a program involves a challenging start. A bumpy start isn't always a danger sign and may be an opportunity for growth. Knee replacement, for example, involves a painful procedure and effortful physical therapy but increases mobility and reduces pain for the long term. Some programs take time, and professionals should be able to explain to parents what is happening and why it's bumpy.

Sometimes a relationship is simply a matter of bad timing or a bad fit. Both parents and professionals can make mistakes. Sam's experience with the audiologist shows that a graceful exit isn't always necessary. However, when the troubles can't be fixed, parents may find that a graceful exit can be a little less soul-robbing than walking out the door and never going back. A graceful exit gives us the chance to acknowledge the conflict and show respect to the other person and the other ways we are connected to each other. The world is a small place, smaller than we think. We may be glad we didn't leave scorched earth behind when someone re-emerges later in our lives with another chance to connect and work with our child to make progress.

We can also walk away from extraneous battles, such as righting wrongs or getting money back, because those battles tend to drain our time and resources for very little in return.

To determine whether a situation needs more time or an exit strategy, and to figure out how best to follow through, we can find help and ideas from someone who has already walked that path. Advocacy and peer groups such as Parent-to-Parent help with information, ideas, and training. A friend or family member who also loves our child can help us think things through. We look for connections that help keep us on the right path.

Scouting for Places of Connection

Wanting to be free. Wanting to be me. Trying to make people see. And accept the real me.
- Scott Lentine

Starting when our child is young, we scout for places to help them grow. We can seek environments and communities rich with possibilities for progress. Some parents may feel barriers to reaching out, such as language differences, lack of resources, or other stigma. To help build strength and resilience in these connections, we can take our first steps toward the most welcoming places. Our first expedition into the world, for example, might be a mother's day out program, a church nursery school, a rec center program, or an inclusive preschool specifically designed to help children with autism learn the social dance of childhood. Structured, inclusive preschools can accelerate learning for all children because children with and without autism have more in common than not. In her work with intentionally designed, inclusive lab schools at Emory University, Gail McGee has created programs that build learning opportunities in the natural environments of childhood. This includes ways for children to learn to talk, imitate, and play. Using the children's interests, the preschool staff combine these rich environments with purposeful orchestration of activities. The programs begin in toddlerhood and progress to kindergarten. If we find such a program with proven effectiveness nearby, we can enroll our child.

Karmel, a master block builder, was one of the many toddlers Shahla watched flourish in a program that replicated McGee's programs. He loved blocks and found kids to share and develop his interests and skills. And teachers who made the most of his interests were able to work with him to expand his talking, sharing, self-help skills, and eventually, reading and writing.

This work—scouting the right environments, configuring the best combinations, and then watching our child go out into the world—continues throughout our child's life. Matteo was the youngest of three children, all with autism. During a telehealth consultation, Shahla noticed that Matteo was already imitating his mother's speech patterns and play. Shahla recommended that, in addition to receiving his therapy, he attended a neighborhood day care center with children a bit younger than he. She based her recommendation on the general understanding that when a child can imitate, he's more likely to copy other children around him. Good centers offer rich environments for these opportunities. At the center, Matteo would have the chance to be around other children and learn from them.

For Matteo, however, attending the center didn't go quite as expected. Shahla knew that he was a talented artist, particularly for a five-year-old. Matteo had filled many notebooks with his drawings of emoji and anime characters. The typical day care classroom outfitted with Legos and Tinker toys held little interest for him. This setting wasn't the best configuration for Matteo. The family needed to scout something new for him. Once he joined other children who shared his passion, including a group of older kids who produced their own style of anime, Matteo imitated those children and flourished.

By fourth grade, Ami had one good friend from school. The two of them spent time together playing Pokemon video games and going to Pokemon tournaments. Ami's mother noticed that what he liked most was building the decks so that the Pokemon could do special things. She scouted out the robotics camp at the local university, thinking the activity was similar to Ami's interests and would offer more opportunities. Ami enjoyed robotics camp and made several new friends there. The children went online to play games together and build virtual settings. They continued going to camps and classes together, forming a social community around their shared interest in robotics.

Our scouting positions will change as our child grows and develops skills and as their interests change. As they scout for their own communities in adolescence and adulthood, we start that age-old dance of letting go. It's hard to relinquish the role and step back, even when our child doesn't have a disability. We are always negotiating between caring for them and allowing them to make their own decisions. Our child is becoming an adult, which involves their successes as well as their failures and injuries. When our child starts to walk, we clear the path and remove objects that may cause harm. Then, when they go out in the world, we work with them to navigate as best they can without harm. We want to prevent suffering, but we must also promote growth.

In scouting for her teenage son with autism, Demetria Ennis-Cole took a wraparound approach. Demetria wanted her son to be part of his community. She had long been involved in community service projects. She joined with other parents and youth, including Shahla and her son, to create Team Help. A professor specializing in learning technologies, Demetria had a lot of experience building tech programs for youth. She put those skills to use when creating Team Help. In Team Help, the teenage boys, some with autism and some without, learned to clean garages, mow lawns, serve meals, volunteer for sensory nights at the science museum, make friends, and show love for their community. The boys learned why the work was important, and practiced courtesy and good work habits. They debriefed after each service project.

Because many of the young men were tall, strong, and Black or Brown, their parents also knew that some neighbors and community members could wrongly see the young men as a threat. Team Help served the community and strove to change those misperceptions and prejudices. The program affected how the youth saw themselves (as members of the community) and how the community viewed them (as contributors to the community). As her son grew into adulthood, the scouting changed and the ideas of Team Help were incorporated into another program for young adults, EPIC. The program centers on opportunities for neurodivergent adults, creating experiences to form deeper relationships with peers, to expand their activities, and to help the broader community through service.

As a child, Darby liked to break things. Once he dropped a telephone and destroyed it. After that, Shahla worked with Darby to take things apart with purpose. They put things back together, too. They started with simple toys and worked up to complicated objects. As an adult, Darby went to work for a major computer company, repairing their computers. While neither Shahla nor Darby's parents were thinking about career goals as Darby was smashing things, they respected and channeled his interest in what turned out to be a powerful direction. Shahla later worked with Darby on other life skills that would help his career, such as packing or purchasing lunch and chatting with coworkers in the lunchroom.

Darby's parents watched for support he might need as a young adult, but also started to step back. Darby could explore his own interests and desires and find his own social communities, even while living at home and even when the community wasn't necessarily one that his parents might have scouted. All children, including children with autism, need places where their identity is supported. As young parents, we will scout places for them, knowing that what they need will change over time. We remain observant as they get older. Some of those groups and alliances will be places of solace and comfort as well as of learning and progress.

One day, our child may also want to be a part of a community built around being autistic. If the scouting leads us there, we need to remember to get out of our child's way, which can be hard to do. After years of working with them to adapt and progress, we might feel rejected when they embrace their identity and explore more of the world around them that doesn't include us. But we can take heart that we probably aren't being rejected. Rather, they are reaching toward their own places in the world. Adolescence and early adulthood come with gray areas as needs and expectations change. Both parent and child have to figure out what's next.

Connecting with Intention

If we are not capable of humanity, we will not have the capacity for joy, for only humanity can destroy the egocentricity that makes joy impossible.
- Thomas Morton

෴

No parent raises a child alone because our community connects us. We weave a new fabric around our family as we join with people who share our concern for our child. Such intentional groups, called communities of practice, share a passion for progress and learning how to make progress.

We need information and honest feedback that may be hard to hear sometimes. With strong, reciprocal relationships built on care and respect, the tough feedback gets easier for us to accept. It's more manageable, too, when we can see both the big picture and the little picture within our mission. In the big picture, we think about the kind of life we want to shape with our child. Within that frame, we consider who our child is and what is required to bring their life forward. We seek out and choose collaborators, make alliances, and scout opportunities. From day-to-day snapshots, we monitor our actions and attitudes, constantly adjusting to keep progress moving. We can remain hopeful.

Some friends, family members, and professionals will always be our collaborators and allies. Groups that offer occasional trusted counsel may shift outcomes for us. Parent-to-Parent, for example, can support what families of children with disabilities need: dealing with logistics, overcoming financial challenges, and managing all the stuff—toys, communication devices, wheelchairs. There's a good chance that an older, wiser parent has dealt with a similar problem and can be a successful match for us.

We will find help in many different places. Peggy often finds books to be places of connection. She will empty the library shelves in search of the author whose perspective can broaden her own. There may be less danger in the information in books compared to information found on the internet. Outliers live on websites, videos, and chat groups where they can appear mainstream (but are not). Unless self-published, books are scrutinized by editors (and by peers on occasion) before a publishing house invests in printing and distributing them.

Some alliances grow into long-term relationships; some don't. A fellow professor, Alicia was Shahla's colleague at first. But over many years, they connected over personal and parenting matters, too. Trina, mother to one of Shahla's first clients when Shahla was a graduate student, stayed connected through the years. Trina called Shahla when her son was struggling with puberty. The support went in the other direction as Shahla's mother was diagnosed with dementia and Trina shared her insights.

Family members can be collaborators and allies. Because the love within a family is deep and trusted, their advice and help nearly always find a place. Shahla's aunts are so close to her in age that they are more like older sisters. When Shahla's children had struggles similar to those of their cousins, her aunts offered abundant advice and wisdom. Peggy's parents stepped in when she and Mark needed respite or fresh perspective, and were especially strong after Mark died. When the children were young, their grandparents' visits included extra help around the house. They tackled at least one project—painting a few rooms, screening part of the porch, organizing the garage—that made life a little easier for their daughter and grandchildren.

Peggy and Shahla have formed deep connections as they continue to grapple with death, job loss, caring for a sick parent, and life's joys and traumas that their children experience. Even in writing this book, examining and talking about all their different experiences—some still painful years later—they found new ways to listen and support each other.

Every person will have different experiences, vantage points, and ways of approaching an issue that can contribute to our strength and resilience, just as our experiences and vantage points contribute to their strength and resilience. In a community of practice, the strength lies in our shared dedication to the mission and to the learning of how to honor and serve a child's life.

We are not alone. Our many connections are a bridge to love.

Part Three: The Power of Loving

Love is like the sea. It's a moving thing, but still and all, it takes its shape from the shore it meets, and it's different with every shore.
- Zora Neale Hurston

෫

Love can bring a boundless capacity to our work with our child. Together with learning, love powers the choices we make. It nurtures deeper meaning in our connections to each other. It guides our actions toward care and kindness so that we can better support our child's hopes and dreams. Sometimes fear, ignorance, or isolation will hamper our ability to tap this power, but love waits for us and is always reachable.

Something deep within tells us that love is essential to life. We grew up in its warmth long before we learned the words to describe it. As adults, we have borrowed the words of philosophers and poets to describe this animating force, for describing love can be like describing water. The Apostle Paul wrote about love in his letter to the Corinthians, a Bible passage so endearing that it has entered pop culture. He wrote that to love is to be patient and kind, humble and content, to protect and trust, to remain hopeful and forgiving, and to be slow to anger and not keep a record of wrongs.

Love also rejoices in the truth, Paul wrote. Our love for our children should be easy, and it often is. Yet, our feelings can also be laced with grief, anger, disappointment, shame, anxiety, and fear. Our needs and expectations can surprise us and catch us unprepared. This is true for loving any child, not just a child with autism. We want to love unconditionally, so we persevere.

Throughout this section, we show how our loving, joyful intentions, whether we are a parent or a professional, can multiply in the world around our child. Professionals and parents have the same capacity for kind and supportive actions—the kindness and support that is essential for everyone's success. When we focus on responding to and helping each other—how we approach and talk with each other, how we learn about and understand each other, how we bring meaning to our interactions—we are tapping the power of love.

In this section, we also shed light on the complicated emotions that can surface in love's dark side. For any family, a diagnosis of autism can test the ways we give and receive love. Moreover, some families don't start out with the same access to resources that others have. These varying conditions have become more transparent as people speak out, particularly people in communities that are marginalized. In all conditions, the power of learning, connecting, and loving applies as we work for the most constructive, least restrictive pathways for progress. The stories in this section illustrate how we can meet our responsibilities for our child's basic care and need for attention and how some families have learned to expand the possibilities for justice.

At the end of this section we see, through the examples of nurturing and making meaning, how other families found their own hearts and souls through their attention to one another and their efforts to move forward. They forged happiness through understanding and action, through the power of responsiveness and science in uncertain times, and through the direction and purpose they found in their work.

Love is among the few things that are not fragile in our changing world. Working together with kindness, patience, and compassion is always a great bet. Love gives us the courage to forge through troubles and find paths toward progress. We know we will fail sometimes, but when we reflect with grace on those failures, our attachments to one another can deepen as we gain understanding and create new meaning. These connections will help us through periods of being unlovable ourselves or of not liking our child.

Love gives life meaning. Love makes a family and a community. We can learn to keep choosing love, above all. We can live in moments of joy.

Joy

Joy gives us wings! In times of joy our strength is more vital, our intellect keener, and our understanding less clouded. We seem better able to cope with the world and to find our sphere of usefulness.
- Abdul-Baha

ۻ

"Up, up and awaaay!" All three family members said it at once, laughing. Chavelo's mother bent over and pulled her toddler close to her feet, tucking her hands under his arms and around his torso. She looked up toward her husband and the camera, broke into a grin, and turned back to look at her son.

"Ready?" she said, smiling eagerly.

Chavelo looked up at her and said "Up . . ." Then he, too, looked up at the camera toward his father before looking back up at his mother to say his version of "away." She squealed with satisfaction at his words and his gaze, swinging him back and forth under the protection of her long legs and out into space. The little boy had the lopsided grin that kids often get when they are proud of something they did and know everyone else is, too. The father cheered from behind the camera. As Chavelo's mother set him back on the floor to start another round, the little boy clapped his hands. This was a fun game.

What happened in this moment was important for many reasons: Chavelo had begun talking; his parents were learning when to help him with prompts and how to fade those prompts and let him fly on his own; they were learning how to break up activities so they would reinforce and encourage his happy progress; they were learning how to make and analyze videos to help them all improve; and they were learning that it was exciting to share such moments with their team. Each one of those things is essential to make progress. Each brought meaning to the moment and, woven together, made a family that was happy together and eager to share that happiness with their community.

Shahla has seen many short, joyful home videos from the families she's worked with over the years. These happy moments initially look almost magical. They are, but that joyful magic was usually created with planning and purpose. Parents and professionals can learn to approach and play with their autistic child with intention. Our child can and should make happy progress at home, school, and the clinic. Making short videos of such moments in all these places creates additional opportunities for us to learn more about what the interactions mean as well as to ask questions and discuss what we might do next. Joyful moments go by fast. Video clips can help us observe all the little things that are happening so we can find ways to expand the moments and the joy.

Consider a father roughhousing on the floor with his preschooler and an oversized pillow. The father raises the pillow high above his head and says "Pop!" To the boy's laughter and delight, the father drops the pillow on top of the boy and gently wiggles it as the boy rolls from side to side. After a few rounds, the father raises the pillow and looks at his son expectantly. The boy looks up to say "Pop!" Down comes the wiggly pillow. They continue the game until the father gets a little winded. After all, it is a big pillow. He sits back on his knees for a moment, breathing heavily but smiling and laughing. He asks his son if he is getting tired. But the boy, still smiling, rolls back over to look up at his dad again and points to the pillow with his eyebrows raised. Dad recovers his energy as quickly as he can. His son has learned new sounds, and he has learned a game that motivates him and teaches him how to time the learning. They are both having fun.

The father understood that this game encouraged his son's speech. But he also recognized the moment as one of the first times that his son tried to keep their interaction going. Dad was learning how to arrange happy activities so that the two of them could move together in harmony. He learned the principles of responding to his son, with help from the team. He knew how to approach his son with kindness, how to encourage his son to approach him, and how to keep that momentum. He understood the importance of his son's assent in whatever activity they did together. He also recognized his son's agency—the ability to act independently and choose freely—as well as his own agency as they learned to move together in the world.

In creating the game of pillow pop, father and son found their own dance. Each moved with their own tune in time and space, and their tunes came together in harmony. When joy guides our choices, each person can be themselves, be together with others, and make progress. We can recognize that individuals may have different reinforcers in a joint activity. We can also recognize the potential to develop and share reinforcers in joint activities. With our strengthening bonds, this may mean simply enjoying being in each other's company.

Consider another example. A mother gently approaches her toddler with a sock puppet. The little boy is sitting on his knees on top of a table, looking out the window, and flicking his fingers in his peripheral vision. She begins to sing a children's song that incorporates different animal sounds, sounds she discovered that her son loves to explore. After a moment, he joins her in making the animal sounds in the song. Then, he turns toward her and gently places his hands on her face. She's singing for him. He reciprocates with his gaze, full of appreciation and tenderness.

Family members might dream of the activities they will enjoy together with their children as they learn and grow. Mothers, fathers, and siblings may not have imagined analyzing videos of themselves singing with sock puppets, playing pillow pop, or creating car-crash bingo games. But these and other examples throughout this book show the possibilities when we open up with intention and learn to enjoy one another's uniqueness and company. Our joy in our child and our family helps us rethink what is easy, what is hard, and what is progress.

All children learn about the way into joyful relationships, and with grace, the dance continues as they grow up. Peggy wondered how the dance would change for Sam in middle school, since she recalled that her own middle school years weren't particularly joyful. Yet, Sam didn't miss one day of class in middle school. The dance had begun with his elementary school classmates, when he belonged to an intentional circle of friends that had already learned to approach one another with care and kindness. Even as they found themselves in a new, sometimes confusing social milieu, even as their bodies shot up in awkward ways, and even as many new experiences vied for their attention, Sam and his classmates shared common ground throughout the day.

This dance of human relationships is one that we all choreograph, first among members of our family, then our schoolmates, and finally, out in the community. Shahla will always remember a film shown by one of her professors, Dr. Judy LeBlanc, from the Anne Sullivan School in Peru. The team there knew they could help a young autistic boy at their school, but he would have to learn to ride the city bus across town by himself, including making several transfers along the way. The team worked out a training program for the boy to learn the way on the city buses, but the training program didn't include anyone in the community at large. Still, the drivers and other passengers got to know the boy, this newest traveling member of their community, and prompted him through the transfers from time to time. Through that shared dance, they amplified the community's relationships.

When joy is present, we recognize the caring approach of others toward us and the need for kindness in our approach toward others. We recognize the mutual assent within our togetherness and the agency each of us enjoys in that togetherness. Joy isn't a material good but an energy found in curiosity, truth, and insight. Once we recognize the bubbling energy that joy brings, we will notice when it is missing and seek it out. Joy occupies those spaces where we are present and looking for the good. Like hope and love, joy is sacred. Moreover, as activist and pastor Nicolas O'Rourke tells us, joy is itself an act of resistance in troubled times.

Walking Through Love's Dark Side

I know it seems hard sometimes but remember one thing. Through every dark night, there's a bright day after that. So no matter how hard it gets, stick your chest out, keep ya head up ... and handle it.
- Tupac Shakur

The responsibilities within the world of autism can be so pervasive and challenging that it's no wonder children, parents, and professionals sometimes buckle under the strain. A generation ago, psychologists blamed autism on so-called "refrigerator mothers," saying that parents were incapable of love. Today we understand more about autism's biological origins. Yet, one reality remains: the label can test the way we receive and give love. Attachments feel somehow bound and tethered to the diagnosis.

Some parents fear their child will be unable to find love in the world around them. We worry that perhaps she cannot love: not her parents, not her brothers and sisters, not her grandparents or teachers, not friends, not even herself. Maybe he'll never find love as an adult, not through friends or coworkers, never dating or getting married.

The dark side of love can bring fear, anger, shame, disappointment, anguish, and grief out into the open. Perhaps we become angry when an extended family member shows impatience. We might feel anguish when neighbors exclude our child from birthday parties and playdates. We worry when a teacher resents the extra effort it takes for our child to master the lessons. We are exhausted by all the work and wonder when we get to enjoy the fun that was supposed to come with parenting. We try to hide our child's oddities. We fret, wondering if they look and act like others, then they can be loved and we can be loved, right?

Love's dark side can disguise itself, too. Sometimes we wear our guilt like a badge of honor, scolding friends and family members who come up short. We might hover over our child and lunge into action at the first sign of discomfort. Some of us may hop from therapist to therapist, blaming them for slow or no progress. Or we stay with a therapist long after progress ends because the relationship is comfortable. Some parents work long hours and travel, feeling they need to make as much money as possible to pay for care. Some withdraw in different ways and leave all the decision-making to others who seem to know better.

The challenges start when an autistic child is young. Some challenges create moments of incredible suffering, and for some families the suffering continues for years. Suffering makes it hard to see beyond the adversity. Suffering can make it hard to be loving toward others, too. The rest of the world often isn't always prepared for our problems, including the social systems meant to help us. What's more, some individuals are oblivious to our suffering, or worse, ready and willing to extend it. We could self-destruct with all this weight on our backs. Instead, we can see our suffering and the emotions clustered around it as flags for learning more about the conditions of distress and as signals of the need to move in a new direction.

Peggy thought she was prepared for the news when the pediatrician first diagnosed Sam. Yet, the announcement still struck a blow. Her swirling emotions signaled a sharp turn ahead for Sam's life, out in an unknown direction. She heard little of the rest of what the pediatrician and the social worker had to say that day. We tend to walk through all the possible horrors at such moments. That's important work. But afterward, we must decide our next steps. The day after the diagnosis, the entire family met the social worker at the university's preschool. Peggy's head was a little clearer that day, and she could observe, hear, and absorb much more information. At the preschool, she saw the possibilities for Sam, especially if the next steps brought him into such a rich environment filled with such loving teachers and therapists and nurtured a plan for progress.

As the years go by, we might find ourselves resenting or envying the regular lives and beautiful children of families around us. One parent, Evelyn, scrolls through social media and feels a pang as cousins and old friends lament the difficulties of college admissions. She knows they are expressing valid feelings, but she wonders whether she will ever worry about college admission for her child with autism. She wonders whether her friends and family appreciate having such anxiety.

Jealousy can be wanting what someone else has or fearing the loss of what we have, but little joy comes from making comparisons. Instead, we can begin to shift our notions about acceptance. Who do we want to accept our child? What are acceptable community values and standards? Young adults with autism have their own perspectives of what is acceptable and valuable. Our child may adopt these perspectives as they grow, from accepting a simple notion that a young man's unshaven face is attractive to far more complex values, such as honoring the fluidity in someone's gender identity and expression.

With some reflection, we may discover that our perspective is shifting already. Consider Cassie, a mother whose job often took her out of town. While on one assignment, her son fell and suffered a deep cut on his face. The physician did a poor job stitching the injury. Cassie fretted for a long time that her beautiful child, who did not have autism, was now scarred for life. Some years later, her daughter lost a thumbnail after dropping a scrap pipe in the family's garage. The on-call doctor looked at the beautiful little girl and her elegant mother in front of him. He decided he ought to manage the family's expectations about how the nail would heal—perhaps never fully and always a bit ugly. He didn't know the family, but his face and voice conveyed the burden. In that moment, Cassie recognized how much her perspective had changed. Her youngest son had autism. His early intervention program took a lot of time and energy, but the family's greatest joys came in hearing his sweet voice as he learned to talk. She thanked the doctor for the insight into her daughter's injury and assured him that avoiding infection and pain was job one.

People around us may still offer unsolicited opinions about our lives and how to be a better parent. Sometimes those opinions can aid our perspective. Sometimes we smile at unsolicited opinions just to get along.

And sometimes we wish people would shut their mouths and keep their judgments to themselves. Anyone can get pulled into a vortex of fear and anger when a child with autism is continuously picking their skin, refusing to use the toilet, or saying a word or phrase over and over. When we feel the judgment of those around us, or we're tired and frustrated, we might resort to whatever we can do to make the seemingly bad behavior stop. Such shortcuts are often costly, although we may not understand why.

Beginning with his parents and continuing with other people throughout his life, Sam has watched family, friends, and strangers do countless things because they were afraid of him. It's not clear when he came to this understanding, but he did so long before he told Peggy about it. He realized that people would not always approach him with an open mind or kindness. His experiences made him wise to the problems that can follow him when people are afraid. As an adult, Sam moves through the world in gentle, calm ways that allow others to keep their fears in check around him. Other people with autism have written about this wisdom, including Temple Grandin, Donna Williams, and even Naoki Higashida, who was just thirteen years old when he wrote *The Reason I Jump*. (See the bibliography for more information on these books).

Fear, anger, shame, anxiety, and despair can often exert more power than feelings of attachment and contentment do. Yet, when these dark emotions come, we can take note. Professor Israel Goldiamond described our emotions as flags that say, "Hey, look around here!" Emotions tell us about the contingencies for ourselves, our children, and our community. For example, fear might tell us that that there is a dangerous condition and someone may hurt our child. Meanwhile, anger might tell us that there is a threat to our child and they will need our protection. Anxiety, that we are unsure of expectations or that the things required of us are conflicting. Envy indicates that we want something someone else has and that we have powerful feelings to unpack and reflect upon. Relief tells us that something difficult has been managed or a bad situation has ended. Lastly, joy reminds us that we have made the most of a moment, we like what's happening, and our children like it, too.

One of Shahla's students, Regan Garden, was interested in this role of emotions and chose it for her thesis topic. She designed a workshop to help clinicians learn about the role of emotions in their work with families. She and the other behavior analysts-in-training studied the many descriptions of emotions, including which are most cherished and pursued. They also considered emotions across many cultures. Using Goldiamond's theory, they discussed what specific emotions might mean about the conditions of the people experiencing them. They looked at dozens of video clips of family interactions and talked about them. Through the process of watching and talking with one another, they learned to see and describe a wider range of emotions than they did before the workshop. They also learned to consider the contingency signals that emotions send.

When emotions fall like dominos, it can be hard to see the signs. For the first few years of Sam's life, Peggy's family lived with considerable fear. As an infant, Sam did not meet his parents' gaze. Holding Sam provided no comfort when he cried. He laughed at spinning wheels and flipping light switches but not at people's funny faces. When out for a walk in the neighborhood or at the park, Sam bolted ahead and never looked back to see if anyone stayed close by. Over weeks and months, a fear of the unknown slowly descended on family members like billions of water droplets, a dense and immobile fog that surrounded them and isolated them for several years.

They moved to Rochester, New York, for a year when Sam was four years old. Mark stayed at home with the children as Peggy attended graduate school. Mark coached Sam to recognize the new daily routine by announcing "Mom's home!" when she returned for lunch. As Peggy opened the front door to their walk-up flat one day, Sam ran to the top of the stairwell and leaned over the child-protection gate to see. He called out "Mom's home!" Sam's cheery description was a declaration of love. A small routine of new family connections had begun: each day, he ran to the stairwell and called out "Mom's home!" Everyone in the family, even baby Michael, echoed out "Mom's home!"

That sunny moment, and many more of them, began easing the family back into the light. Once we can see what our emotions signal, we have more clues to figure things out and come up with a plan. Sam loved his family. But they needed to better recognize how he expressed his attachment to them, like that echo from the top of the stairs.

Later, the family invited a therapist with Lekotek, an international nonprofit that serves children with disabilities, to visit once a month. The therapist experimented with different toys, finding what captured Sam's attention, and began to foster his learning through play. She, too, worked with the family to connect to one another in new ways. Both parents and siblings learned how to respond to Sam so that everyone better perceived and received one another's loving messages.

There are no easy answers here. Behavior analysts, counselors, friends, and siblings can help us examine our darker emotions and think through needed changes. But the emotions are ours. Answers come from a deep understanding of where we came from and the conditions of the path we are on as well as the path our child is on. We also develop that understanding by being mindful and watching the emotional barometers in ourselves and our family. Our learning about contingencies can help us find the way forward, too. The stimuli that happen before and during our feelings will give us clues about what we can accept or change. There is an area of behavior analysis called Acceptance and Commitment Therapy (ACT) that helps families meaningfully explore these issues.

Our paths will likely be different from those around us, even from the paths of other autism families. Still, we can ask a more experienced parent about organizing playdates, riding lessons, and gaming nights. We can develop strategies to redirect impatient family members or limit their time with our child. We can volunteer at school. We find a friend to step in when we don't have the fortitude. We figure out how to work together with the teacher to make behavior plans, rather than being at odds with them. We make time to talk through our concerns about our child's future. When we let our emotions signal to us that something has to change, we can tap our circle of friends and collaborators to puzzle it out. Finally, if our fears take over, if the fog is too dense and too persistent, if we are angry all the time—and especially if we act on that anger—we seek specialized help.

We do this so that we can learn and make progress along with our child. We do this so we can spend more time under the conditions that feel good to us and to our beloved children. We do this so that others can see the good side of the world of autism, as we are learning to do.

Like Sam's Lekotek therapist, professionals are paid to work with us, but their intentions can remain sincere. Renowned behavior analysts decided long ago that their scientific study must be both objective and socially relevant. Behavior analyst Montrose Wolf, for example, wrote that research and clinical work in human behavior must be grounded in a responsibility that moves away from the dark side of despair and apathy and toward qualities humans care about the most, like love and joy. This responsibility came with action and that action involved recognizing the pain and difficulty, imagining a different way, and then creating it. This work involves a big dose of caring about our child and their future.

Some professionals worry that becoming attached to their clients can cloud their thinking and make them cross forbidden boundaries. Yet, attachment and detachment are not opposing forces in human relationships. Detachment improves our objectivity in observing human actions and in learning. Parents can use detachment, too. As we see our child's autism with increasing clarity, we can also reinforce our attachment to them and our love for them. Being loving and being detached are not mutually exclusive qualities—for either parents or professionals.

When Jamal was two years old, he spent most of his time running in circles around the house, opening and closing doors, stacking Golden books, making the same noise over and over. He interacted very little with his parents. He would even run away when they looked at him. It would have been easy for his parents and the professional team to take a darker view and see Jamal as a series of things to fear, fix, stop, or eliminate. Instead, they chose to center on connecting with him. The first step was finding a connection point.

Shahla and the rest of the team saw that Jamal liked to be tickled, which offered that connection point. He would pull on his parents' hands to get them to tickle him. His parents would oblige, often tickling him until either they or Jamal got tired of it. Then Jamal would walk off to stack books or open and close doors again. To Jamal's parents, the tickling didn't feel like a loving interaction. They felt as if they served as a useful set of hands to their toddler.

Shahla and the rest of Jamal's therapy team saw that tickling offered an opening, an opportunity for Jamal and his family to move toward love. They showed Jamal's parents how to stop tickling for a few seconds and wait for Jamal to respond. When Jamal reached for their hand, they would start tickling him again. Bit by bit, they would wait for more social interaction. First, they would wait for Jamal to turn his body toward theirs, and later for him to turn his face toward theirs, before tickling him again. Then, Jamal's mom introduced a new way of tickling: blowing raspberries on his belly. That made Jamal laugh, which allowed her to lengthen other social interactions with him. Sometimes when he simply looked at her, she made the sound. Jamal would laugh and continue to look at her to see what she would do next.

Together, the therapists and parents worked with Jamal to broaden the ways he showed interest in and increased his attention to the people around him. Not only did these changes help Jamal learn, but they also increased the communication and feelings of connection among family members. This small series of interactions and the opportunities that they created were probably a cusp. As Jamal and his family learned, they transformed. Jamal expanded his skills and his world, his parents learned ways to broaden the complexity of his actions, and the discomfort that they felt dissipated.

This applies at all levels. As Lutzker and Campbell tell us, the child is part of family and community systems. Parents and professionals can benefit from turning away from contention and towards connection. No matter where we start, when we start with loving goals, we can build a more meaningful life as we work toward those goals. A goal for warring parents to have a regular night out, for example, may seem like building a pleasant life rather than a meaningful one. But for the couple working toward a deeper relationship, a regular night out helps build a loving family. The purpose of a teacher-parent meeting may be to review and agree on a child's special education plan. Rather than a battle, it can include getting to know each other during the meeting, whether it's each other's communication styles, values, perspectives, or finding out what everyone sees as important. A deeper, more loving collaboration can give all the adults on a child's special education team a better chance at achieving important goals and living a more meaningful life.

When a dark emotion emerges, we can pause, regroup, and search for a productive response. When we feel anxious, for example, we are seeing conditions we didn't expect. Our anxiety tells us that we need information to find and take those next steps. When we feel guilty, we may be avoiding a task that needs to be done. If that step is something within our control, then we line up the assistance we need. Guilt can also emerge over things that aren't in our control, in which case the emotion flags a perspective that's misplaced—a mother who feels guilty that she did something during pregnancy to cause her child's autism, for example.

We may be clumsy when we first try a new way or response. That's okay. Parents of children without disabilities often find it easier to try new things because their children are more resilient. And the world may not be ready for our new, different ways. Our family may be less resilient, but we can also trust that our child will recognize our caring and kindness as we try different ways of responding to them.

Trying new things can also be tough if we lack collaborators and allies to model and problem-solve with us. We're all afraid of the unknown. We need good, knowledgeable help when we are afraid and lack skills. Without it, we are more likely to punish our child (and ourselves). Most parents don't want to punish, but the short-term relief that follows punishment makes it easy to slip into a pattern. We may not recognize the pattern or the relief. But that brief break increases the likelihood that we will take the shortcut again. Frequent shortcuts hurt our long-term relationship with our child. They will start avoiding us in myriad ways. Our relationship will deteriorate into one based on coercion. We can approach each other with trust and determination, instead. That way, we'll find our path through frustration together.

As we pick up better ideas and skills, we will experience new responses to our new actions. We can adjust our responses to be more effective in whatever way is important to our family. We will have to do some things, maybe many things, in different ways. Perhaps, for example, we are working with our child to feed themselves without our assistance. To enjoy a dinner out, then, we must prepare in a different way. Perhaps we must pack up a special spoon and plate to bring to the restaurant. The prep work takes time and effort and feels uncomfortable. That's because we are doing something hard. We are relearning something we thought we knew. But we have permission to relearn time and again, a new learning curve that accelerates over time. Above all, we are showing our child how much we love them in ways that may seem small but are substantial.

We may feel like our lives are not going to be "normal." We will often need to face a world that has been arranged for others but not for our child. For example, our child may respond to early intervention and learn to talk, or they may not. Then, we must communicate through sign language or a picture board, instead.

We may recognize that even among the children that flourish with that early work, adaptation to a world arranged for others is not the same as asking a child to conform to it. Stefan's mother was one parent who recognized this. Stefan liked to twirl things, but Shahla noted that by middle school, he became self-conscious about twirling in front of others. One day he came home from school and politely asked his mother if he could retreat to his closet to twirl hangers. On one hand, the activity was harmless and an odd thing to seek permission for. On the other hand, he was learning that there are things his family chose to do in front of people and things they didn't. Stefan's request was a turning point for the family and became a lesson in negotiating the boundaries of etiquette with love.

We can take comfort in knowing that our child has their own soul and their own path—a lesson all parents master at some point but one we might master a little sooner. When our burden is heavy, when fear looms large and makes us doubt what to do next, we can focus on guiding principles and what produces progress. We think about what the priorities are at that moment (communicating when we are late, for example), the boundary lines (acknowledging that one-sided conversations aren't considerate), and who can help on this journey (asking a grandfather for rides to the new play sessions).

Our growing knowledge and skills allow us to teach new things, connect with our child, and lead a more aware, purposeful life. We see how our child loves and feels loved. We understand our own emotions related to our child. We begin to understand the support from our community or why it is lacking. We usually can't change the behavior of others around us, but when we change our own, we can be confident that may inspire others to change. And if we start each day fresh, as if yesterday's hurts were good lessons, we will find those bits of love growing in our child's world.

By remaining humble and hopeful, family members can better attach to one another. Autism forces all of us to examine which human behaviors are and are not important and how we can approach our collective progress. We see that our child is attached to us and loves us and feels our love in return, even if this love is different from other children's affections. The evidence may come in unexpected ways and in unexpected places. Joy allows us to fully experience these sunlit, loving moments.

Learning to Love

Love isn't a state of perfect caring. It is an active noun like struggle. To love someone is to strive to accept that person exactly the way he or she is, right here and now.
- Fred Rogers

❧

Autism sometimes asks us to stop and rethink the many joyful, nurturing actions that would otherwise have been second nature to us. An autism diagnosis likely changes how we respond, but we are still parenting. Providing for our child's safety and basic care may require more of us than we anticipated.

Autistic children are vulnerable to harm and in unexpected ways. Parents must sometimes stay vigilant beyond a child's first few years. Some toddlers are brilliant escape artists. Some children wander when they get older, isolating themselves and avoiding help from others. Some children suffer the relentless taunts of bullies. Some are molested. And perhaps no interaction can be higher stakes than one with a police officer. While conditions in many community police departments are changing, not all law enforcement officers have trained to recognize, communicate, and respond appropriately to people with autism. To protect an autistic individual as they become part of the broader community, parents, professionals, and caregivers should consider connecting with local law enforcement.

Demetria visits the local police department once or twice each year to talk with officers about her son and how his autism affects him. She leaves, in a plastic sleeve, an updated photo with helpful information along with family contact information so that the information can be part of the department's resources. After her son got his driver's license, the department added that information to its databases. Demetria says this outreach has protected her son, as he has been stopped three times in recent years. Once he had a small red jar of bubbles in his hands. Another time, he was listening to music on a small voice recorder. The third encounter came the first time he drove at night: he forgot to turn the car lights on. On each occasion, the officers recognized that they had detained Demetria's son and had the information they needed to interact with him.

Demetria says the continuing support helps, particularly when her son visits adjacent neighborhoods where the family is less well known, and when he is among individuals who, sadly, have come to think of every stranger as a threat.

To best protect their child, parents can think ahead about the risks their child's autism presents, and scout for resources to minimize those risks rather than succumbing to vague fears about their child's vulnerabilities. They can implement strategies to deal with escaping and wandering, to guide the child who approaches strangers, to visit the local police department, and more.

Basic protection and care are part of helping any child be accepted and lovable. Parents readily overcome their initial disgust to keep a newborn baby clean and healthy—wiping away spittle, cleaning up vomit, changing diapers, working with others to prevent injury. An autistic child might require this kind of basic care and protection well past toddlerhood, and that care may need adjustments if required through adulthood. Parents love their children fiercely, so they do it.

Professionals should also be ready to provide basic care. When visiting Sam's preschool one day, Peggy noticed that a classmate needed his diaper changed, but neither the special education teacher nor the teacher's aide ever changed the boy's diaper the entire, long morning. This oversight created a problem both for the boy's basic health and for his social well-being. The class joined other children several times a week in another parent-participation preschool on campus. Why would a teacher send a child with a dirty diaper to play with other children? For whatever reason—disgust, overwhelmed by daily responsibilities, or something else—the decision to ignore a dirty diaper is a form of social rejection and sets a child up to be rejected by others.

Disgust can be a powerful emotion. In cross-cultural studies, researchers have found that human beings share this reaction to bodily products and injuries as well as to signs of disease and decay. For self-preservation, humans respond to disgust by stopping or moving away. But there is more. Entire cultures are shaped through social expectations, which means that other situations can trigger disgust, too. We might decide that some social expectations are unreasonable, and defy them for our child's integrity and well-being, but we don't have carte blanche to ignore them all. All children learn what it means to be a social being from their parents, the rest of their families, and the community around them. Human beings have always valued and expected important behaviors that contribute to the well-being of the whole human family. When possible, toileting is one such expectation. Personal hygiene also matters, so we can work with our child to meet these expectations. Researchers at Princeton Child Development Institute developed an index to help identify expectations of cleanliness and basic attention to physical care and then used this information to help their students with autism meet community expectations.

There are behaviors common to some children with autism that trigger other kinds of disgust. Children might pick their skin until it scabs or regurgitate their food, both of which can create odor. Less-jarring behaviors can also trigger disgust depending on cultural expectations. The norms of some social circles are strident, or superficial, but failing to meet them will still trigger disgust among that circle's members.

When we feel discomfort or disgust, we may fail to see that we aren't connecting to another human being, which is part of surviving and thriving. When disgusted, we can be inhumane. This tragedy plays out in some families when one parent feels shame and disgust and blames the other parent for their autistic child's behavior. When repelled by a child's behavior, a professional can compound the tragedy. We may watch in dismay as a professional fails to recognize their disgust and rejection of our family and our child, rather than creating a space to support change.

Without knowledge or skills, we may not know how to enter a situation when we are repelled. We struggle to find a kinder response. Shahla consulted with a family whose thirteen-year-old daughter needed help with toileting. Several interventions over the years had failed; to compound matters, many of the things she loved to do were ruined after being linked inappropriately to her various toilet training programs. Before getting started, Shahla insisted that the girl be evaluated by a doctor. The doctor found that her bowels were compacted and had created other complications, such as halitosis, adding to the girl's suffering and isolation. Her medical treatment followed a gentle path that took nearly a year to complete. But while that unfolded, the team also built rapport with the girl and helped her re-establish her communications and relationships to others. With those fundamentals in place—and her suffering relieved—she responded to the toileting program with ease.

Adolescence brings its own collection of changes that can trigger disgust in others—surging hormones, growing bodies, stronger smells, an interest in sex. We may also face people who remain prejudiced about the sexuality and physical appearance of individuals with disabilities. We have a long way to go in understanding and responding to one another. Sometimes the community changes, other times the child changes. In the best of cases, everyone changes and progress follows collaboration.

We may not have bargained on the fact that basic nurturing is a skill. Having a child with autism may limit some choices, but we can support them to expand their choices as much as possible. Parents benefit from being thorough and deliberate through many facets of their children's lives. Sometimes we will do this quite well; other times we do it poorly or give up altogether.

In the same vein, we don't have to be bewildered by the science behind our child's treatment. We'll discover that the more we learn the skills and the more effectively we collaborate, the more our lives have deeper meaning and purpose. When things go awry, our growing wisdom and love's animating force can help us right ourselves.

Love's existence may be a law of nature, but the knowledge and skills developed in nurturing love will deepen the attracting force between parent and child, between brother and sister, among family members, among friends, among us all.

The Sunshine of Our Attention

Do small things with great love.
- Mother Teresa

We are born as loving beings. Our baby shows her desire to survive and to thrive as she looks into our eyes. We return her gaze with love. Through our eye contact, we convey that we are on her side. We seek one another; we amuse one another with our shared gazes. Eye contact is a primal, unspoken, beautiful way that we begin to connect with each other and communicate. We see each other; we convey meaning; we create a world together; we sustain each other's vitality.

This fundamental dance is often awkward or missing for a child with autism. She possesses that same desire to thrive even though eye contact is difficult, perhaps impossible, for her to achieve. Without that intangible asset, she will likely miss thousands of little cues from people around her, beginning with her own family. Yet, her desire to survive and thrive remains. Without that intangible bond, her parents may not recognize they have disconnected. Yet, their desire to love, protect, and nurture remains.

We work with our child to find new ways to connect to each other and convey meaning. As we look for those new ways to connect, we reinforce that loving space and all that it means between us. We make those extra connections strong, which creates the possibility for more connections. We build new bridges toward each other and find love where it is.

The best interventions create those connections by design. The work progresses from programs that teach simple social initiations, such as exchanging preferred toys and imitating one another, to conversation, negotiation, and teaching others. For some children, eye contact and other traditional ways of connecting will prevail. Beauty rises from our loving gaze and focused attention, letting our child know that we love them. For other children, parents and professionals may need to find alternative ways to connect and nourish relationships.

We may not always give our full attention to all the ways that we connect and reinforce meaning with each other. In addition, we may not always realize when we aren't connecting. Paying attention to how we love our child can be a lot of work. Yet, our attention is like water and sunshine. Wherever we give it, things will grow.

One semester, Shahla taught a class on behavioral approaches in parent training. The curriculum included Glenn Latham's book, *The Power of Positive Parenting*. A student in the class was also the mother of a fourteen-year-old girl. As the semester progressed, the student began to see how stormy her parenting relationship was. Her daughter yelled a lot, slammed doors, walked off during conversations, and stayed isolated in her room. The mother recognized that she often criticized and reprimanded her daughter, which triggered more yelling and slamming from her daughter.

The mother started to apply what she was learning in class by shifting her responses at home. She poured the water and sunshine of her attention toward reinforcing whatever small thing she could—a smile, a kind word, any small thing that was positive from her daughter. She coached herself away from attending to things that were going wrong. If her daughter was calm while watching television, she put her hand on her daughter's shoulder for a moment. If her daughter walked to the dinner table with a neutral face, she smiled at her. She told Shahla that after several weeks of pivoting her attention away from the trouble spots, the storm between her and her daughter calmed quite a bit. She made progress within herself, too. She realized what a wonderful person her daughter was and how much she loved her.

This sunshine-of-our-attention metaphor applies in many places that storm clouds gather. Trouble often follows the child who has not yet developed communication skills and healthy ways to connect with others. When we cannot connect and communicate with our child, we both may be in pain. We want to make the pain stop. Our natural response is to "shout away" things that make us uncomfortable. However, when we communicate with force, we risk becoming aggressive and aversive in both physical and emotional ways, shouting away our relationships. When we can keep ourselves from being blown about, we are better able to select the conditions that serve our family well in the long run. We can move out of storms and into the light.

Peggy once withheld a freshly baked snickerdoodle from Sam (his favorite) when he was a toddler, thinking it would get him to say "cookie." As the tears welled in his eyes, she saw the cruelty in her actions and handed over the treat. Withholding the cookie wasn't a problem per se, but the steps Sam had to take to get the cookie were way too big. He had few words in his vocabulary, and he rarely said the word "cookie." She was afraid Sam would never talk, but she wasn't willing to lose his trust. We must unhook ourselves from those big balls of fear and frustration by giving attention, instead, to what offers the promise of progress. To do that, we may need to step back for a minute, watch and listen to our child, and then center ourselves to figure out what might work. Don't underestimate the power of taking a deep, calming breath, or casting a loving smile, or handing over the cookie, until the problem—and the solution—come into view.

Sometimes we hit the sweet spot: everything progresses and everyone is happy. Other times, we will bumble along and our child will be okay. And more often than we all would like, our work unravels and everyone is unhappy. Our family's survival also requires us to conserve energy and to allocate resources with wisdom.

Clinicians and researchers have discovered what sustains behavior problems and are applying that knowledge to prevent issues from developing in the first place. This wisdom heads off big problems that can hold our child back, such as hitting themselves or being aggressive toward others, running away, or eating inedible things (pica). If we focus on nurturing our child's communication, skill expansion, and adaptive strategies, particularly when they are young, we can avoid these setbacks. The work helps our child know that we love them and are on their side. And we become confident that we are capable of being on their side.

Nurturing our child's ability to connect and communicate means finding safe ways for them to express their wants, needs, likes, and dislikes in ways that other people understand. Peggy's trust and compassion sustained her and Sam while she learned the incremental steps to shape Sam's communication. Those steps were more attainable for him and less emotionally charged for both of them.

One autistic child, Uku, demonstrated the importance of a family's focused attention to develop communication. Four-year-old Uku's parents and grandparents understood his idiosyncratic combination of sounds and gestures and responded when he was thirsty, tired, hungry, or hurt. But other people didn't understand. His exhausted parents translated his squeals and gestures at family gatherings, among friends, and out in the community. Yet, Uku's limited communication skills kept his older brother, parents, and grandparents from deeper connections with him. As Uku grew, the isolation became more frustrating.

The family reached out to a hospital-based program for help. Uku's team worked first to build a picture exchange system for his communication. Based on the seminal work of Andy Bondy and Lori Frost, these alternative methods ease communication frustrations before more problems emerge and current ones become entrenched. For Uku, the picture exchanges also opened up new possibilities for him to communicate with family members and teachers through more open-ended questions about his wants and needs.

Successful communication between people requires their shared attention to the topic. Whether they have autism or not, all humans struggle for attention on whatever the topic might be, particularly with busy adults. Our child with autism may struggle more. When we respond to each of their positive overtures for our attention, we are welcoming their voice. We can and should do more to work with them to gain the attention of others. For example, if our child learns that tapping someone gently on the shoulder or calling their name works, she may not get in the habit of hitting herself or others or running away in order to gain their attention. We can nurture her understanding of additional, acceptable ways to gain people's attention as she grows.

People may expect different cues for their attention, particularly from teens as compared to younger children. The middle years and adolescence bring their own challenges. Our child will do better when they know how to be a good sport, give compliments, apologize, and ask for help. We can do our best to work with them to see the world from another person's perspective, or at least be able to acknowledge that not everyone sees the world as they do.

Our child also must be able to cope with the challenges that come their way. We can use our attention to show empathy and kindness in situations that our child finds aversive, even if they have no option but to go through those situations. Chances are, they are already coping with challenges that aren't apparent to us. In his book, *The Reason I Jump*, Naoki Higashida wrote that certain noises that appear to go unnoticed by most people bother him and other autistic people. To cope, he cups his ears. "It's not quite that the noises grate on our nerves. It's more to do with a fear that if we keep listening, we'll lose all sense of where we are," he wrote. Certain sights, sounds, or other stimuli can overwhelm the senses the way that food does. Those flooded senses can have different meanings, comfort levels, and controversies for autistic people.

More often than not, our child must go through the struggle that lies before them. Sometimes we can make adaptations on their behalf. Sometimes we can teach skills, whether for our child or the people around them, to bring comfort and ease. Because our child is growing and changing, we watch for what's new or different so that we remain responsive, knowing that our loving capabilities will deepen as we go.

We can nurture a young child's ability to adapt to the world through several strategies. First, we can encourage them to enjoy the downtime of solo play and leisure activities. Introducing the idea of downtime requires some creativity when our child is small, but there are things we can do. Researchers have found, for example, that if we modify our child's play materials a bit, we can encourage new types of play. As a preschooler, Sam enjoyed tipping cars upside down and spinning the wheels. Peggy wasn't sure that the time Sam spent looking at the spinning wheels was always constructive for him. But she could see that Sam was exploring the reliability of his effect on the world, since he would also flip light switches and pursue similar cause-and-effect activities with zeal.

She and Mark decided to build Sam an elevated sandbox, where he could experiment with cause and effect without having to sit in the sand, which was aversive to him. Peggy occasionally changed what was available in the sandbox during the summer, including adding water and water features, such as toy boats and water wheels. Sam enjoyed long play sessions by himself in the sand-and-water box.

Of course, computer games also offer myriad new opportunities to enjoy downtime and to learn while playing. Parents may need to give some time and attention to arranging that play space to make sure the computer games are constructive or at least not dangerous. Almost all of us have a preferred hobby or leisure activity that enriches our lives, and our child may enjoy joining family members or community groups through games, sports, and other pursuits. Researchers have also explored ways to systematically expand interests and activities, and as our child with autism grows they will develop their own hobbies and leisure activities, enriching our family life along the way. For a child who requires support to learn such self-direction, Greg McDuff and researchers at the Princeton Child Development Institute have developed scheduling aides.

Second, kids with autism often have a hard time with transition and change. We can nurture adaptive skills in those situations. We watch for transitions that are difficult for them and find creative ways that our child can learn to be part of a group and have some agency in controlling the flow of the situation. They will know we are on their side, for example, when we lay out true choices for getting dressed, hopping in the car, or going to bed. We also may need to signal schedule changes in plain-spoken ways.

Sam did well with having a written schedule at his desk and a large clock in view during elementary school. According to the school principal, while Sam's first grade teacher was an experienced and successful educator, she was notorious for getting off schedule—that is, until she had Sam as a student. With the day's schedule on his desk, Sam reminded the teacher when it was time to start the math lesson and so forth. The true beauty emerged when she responded with a smile to his prompts, whether she pivoted to the next lesson or announced to the class what needed to be done before they could move on.

Third, by building support into important tasks, we can work with our child to build patience. Researchers Joseph Ducharme and David Worling worked with a five-year-old boy and a fifteen-year-old girl on their ability to follow instructions, by harnessing momentum in their behavior. They set up a series of successful responses that paved the way for tasks the children had not yet mastered. To create the momentum that worked for each child, the researchers set up a sequence of requests that included a difficult task in between easier or more desirable ones. The researchers learned that certain kinds of sequences mattered for each child. When the children had successfully completed the sequences enough times, the harder tasks became easier, in part because plentiful reinforcement kept them in the learning game. With this procedure, our child can learn to follow instructions that were once difficult. They may also develop more patience with tough situations and themselves.

Finally, we can work with our children to learn to tolerate tough situations. Some of that ability comes with growing up. And when our child knows we love them—because we've shown it all along by connecting and communicating—they will trust us and our guidance when life's harder lessons roll by (at least most of the time). Children must forge their own way in order to build spiritual, emotional, and physical strength. Their resilience emerges from accepting those challenging situations and learning how to get through them. That is hard to watch—we want the people we love to not suffer and be comfortable—but growth comes from struggle, too.

Deeper Connections and Progress

If only people freed themselves from their beliefs [of all kinds] the simple law of love, natural to man, accessible to all and solving all questions and perplexities, would of itself become clear and obligatory.
- Leo Tolstoy

One of the wonderful things about life is that we all continue to learn. Humans are amazing, absorbent, malleable beings full of invention, resilience, and love. Parents and children are capable of great advances. Cultivating more options allows us to make progress at any stage and any age. Working with children with autism when they are young is particularly vital to their long-term well-being, but we don't have to give up on learning as our child gets older, either.

A few generations ago, doctors told parents to take their child with autism to a state institution and never look back. Policymakers considered it folly to allocate resources. They didn't understand or believe that people with disabilities were worth time and attention. Sometimes these old ideas come back, and we should not let such notions knock us off our axis. Reliable information and strong connections to our community offer the only adaptable formula for progress and happiness in our changing world.

The broader truth is this: science can inform love, and love can inform science. Love is an attracting force between parent and child, throughout the family, and among friends. Parents and professionals alike can borrow ideas from other disciplines to reveal these connections between a child with autism and the rest of the world and to open up options. For example, wildlife researchers have borrowed dance choreography symbols to study how attachments form between animals. Affection is a complex social behavior. We show affection by giving time, attention, and gratitude. But the whole of our affection may be much more than the sum of the behaviors we use to express them. We, too, can use imaginative ways to collect information to better see how people with autism become attached to others, since those attachments can express themselves in different ways.

In *The Siege*, Clara Park describes how she encouraged her autistic daughter's fullest participation in family life and, thus, her connections to others at a time when other autism services were scant. Park wasn't a scientist in the common way we think of scientists. As an English professor, she was educated in observing and thinking critically about what she saw. Art and literature have long helped people shift their perspective and see new ideas with clarity. Park kept a daily journal, detailing her observations of her daughter and family life. She applied her years of study of language, too, to find more options in her interactions with her daughter. She filled her book with keen observations of language and behavior. She also described studying and altering her own responses to elicit her daughter's progress. What is that, if not a bit of science?

Through her storytelling, Park shared how she shifted perspective to gain more insight from her observations. Along the way, her daughter proved her intelligence in unexpected ways, as children with autism often do. Park showed how she developed options to encourage her daughter's growing independence and to communicate the importance of being a contributing member of the family. The family understood that love consists of learned acts. As Park and her husband aged, their daughter cooked their meals and prepared their medications for them. In this way, the Park's family experience also shows that, no matter the disability, we all can contribute in some way to the responsibility of caring for one another, beginning with our family and extending into our community. Their experience reminds us that fostering reciprocity was key. Teaching loving responses was a core element in building options for Park's daughter. The people around her also had to see the loving possibilities.

The ways to demonstrate our affection aren't always obvious. When our child is being aggressive, for example, we may feel we have little to offer. When someone is hurting us, our attachment to each other can feel like a chokehold. Yet, this also can be one of the places we learn the most about loving: stepping back, learning to manage the sunshine of our attention, and getting help are all ways to love.

We can take heart that some scientists are identifying ways to see and nurture our attachments, even in troubling conditions. In her research, Mary Baker found ways to build the bond between siblings, for example. She capitalized on the strengths inherent in autism, such as a child's fixations, to create bingo games that inspired siblings to play together. Wayne, who was about five-and-a-half years old at the time of Baker's study, could be aggressive. His sister, who was three years older than Wayne, didn't want to play with him. She told the therapists that he was mean and he never listened to her.

Baker and the rest of the team created a bingo game that capitalized on Wayne's fixation with crashing toy cars into each other. Car-crash bingo was a big success. Both Wayne and his sister enjoyed playing car-crash bingo together. The game opened the door for the two of them to learn to play other games together. Throughout the study period, Wayne, the other children with autism, and their siblings connected in new ways through the customized games that Baker and the team worked with them to create. The siblings' time together gave them new ways to demonstrate how they cared for each other.

The team checked on Wayne and his sister after the study ended to see how they were doing. The sister said that she asked Wayne to play games with her on Saturday nights. She said that he was good at pillow games, computer games, and easy board games. She was also working with him to play card games, which he wasn't as skilled at yet. The parents also reported that Wayne and his sister were playing together a little more. And they noted that Wayne's ritualistic behaviors—the source of much of his social rejection and aggression—had diminished since he learned how to play games with other children.

Good intervention design lies at the heart of Baker's research. The games she created built a thoughtful chain of responses that encouraged different ways of reacting to the world, with less dependence on prompts. Master clinicians can bring a child's new behavior into contact with more natural reinforcers, which, in turn, builds bridges of connection to other people.

Within her intervention design, Baker relied on shaping. The concept of shaping is both a metaphor and a description of the technique. Technically, there are different types of shaping, and each contributes to the design of successful interventions. Metaphorically, shaping can be a guiding principle—a way to direct progressively more complex interactions. Both the metaphorical and technical concepts inform a skilled behavior analyst's practice. To shape new behaviors in her study, Baker assessed each child's responses and conditions in their family. She started the program from there. While her research focused on the customized bingo game, we can shape in all kinds of ways.

Moreover, when we are shaping, we are responding to one another. And when our responses come with the kind of thought and care that go into shaping, we are nurturing the love between us and our child as well as the people around them. The concept can be hard to grasp because both parents and professionals often think about actions and responses along a single line—one if-then proposition at a time. Yet, when our shaping is at its best, we cover many dimensions and many if-thens. We change the environment around our child in far more loving ways when we are shaping. We make full use of our imaginations and create many ways of interacting with our child to get where we want to go together.

If we try to keep the environment or the path too narrow, our child will find their own way to respond. Their response tells us we need to adjust. Shahla once witnessed a video of a boy avoiding eye contact in elaborate ways with an unskilled therapist. The boy did not look up when asked. As the therapist put his hands on the boy's face and turned his head toward him, the boy closed his eyes. When the therapist followed that by opening the boy's eyelids with his fingertips, the boy rolled his eyes to the back of his head. The therapist's efforts were unskilled and unethical; the boy did what he could do to escape the situation.

The therapist failed to make sure that each tiny approach the boy made toward him was reinforced. He didn't necessarily have to have eye contact to know that the boy was moving in the right direction. In addition to our child's gaze, we have many ways to tell each other we want to connect, from approaching, pointing, touching, talking, and more. But after that eye-opening interaction, unfortunately, the boy and the therapist had aversive conditions to work through to connect to each other. Force seldom nurtures love or progress.

Instead of creating a restrictive environment, a therapist can arrange responses toward a richer environment that fosters shared attention. The therapist needed to give the boy more choices to shift his attention toward him. With freer conditions and lots of alternatives to respond, a therapist and a child can better adjust to learning together. The best responses will nurture those connections made with our shared attention. More options make a more loving relationship.

For example, to shape the boy's response to the therapist's request for his attention, the therapist works first on moving toward one another. The therapist then works on orienting their heads toward each other, before finally working on eye contact. Some children with autism have no muscles or motivation to understand the shared dance of making contact. In other words, if we start where our child is and leave the path open, a very young child is more likely to develop the learning muscle and sustain the momentum they need to move forward with us. For the older child, it may be too uncomfortable to make eye contact. The shaping process will tell us if we should find other responses. If our child leaves, we need to find a different way. Shaping involves our child's full assent and no forced involvement. When the shaping is done well, the work can result in our unique shared and loving attention to each other and to the world.

When we aren't shaping, we also risk jumping ahead too far, as Peggy did in that brief moment when she withheld the cookie. In both small and large ways, shaping seeks our child's responsiveness to learn from others. We want our child to look at us, and at others, so that we can learn from each other and share reinforcers. We can understand the logic of shaping (even if not all the scientific groundwork behind it) and this notion of incremental progress. We can apply reinforcements and contingencies in systematic ways and measure whether things are getting better. That's the heart of the science that will help our child.

Our child and the environment around them are the most malleable when they are young. During the early years, we strive to be responsive and make the most of this wide open window. We meet this loving demand to nurture our child's potential and opportunities. We gather the information and resources that research tells us will help. We find providers who are well trained in early intervention and can configure our child's world for progress. We are intensive and purposeful in many ways: when communicating with our child, when supporting their social interactions and their play, when working with them on their daily living skills, and when helping them expand their interests.

In the beginning of any child's life, everyone is learning how to learn, including the adults. We are learning how to communicate our expectations to our child: what needs to increase, what needs to dissipate, how to be successful. Autism brings different types of engagement, but they still include the back-and-forth exchanges of human communication and social life. The conditions are just different from a child's typical development and require individual, even unique, arrangements for our child. All parents strive to respond to their children in the most productive, happy ways possible. For our child with autism, we must learn ways of interacting to stay productive and happy, and those ways will likely be different from what we expect. With coaching, we can better learn what best shapes our child's and our own development.

As some autism therapy programs scale up to serve many children at once, some of this knowledge about learning-to-learn programs has gotten lost. Still, many researchers and therapists know that responsiveness is among the most important qualities to teach and foster in parent-child interactions. Researchers Carl Dunst, Carol Trivette, and Deborah Hamby reviewed forty-seven major studies of parent-child training and noted the conditions when a family flourishes: the treatment is family-centered, and the family has learned to be attentive to their children's attempts to be social as well as to their incremental progress. Even in unusual circumstances, family members can learn to create more connections and tap into a cumulative building of one another's capabilities. As a result, family members feel better and happier. That's the love.

Making Meaning and Living the Good-Enough Life

Children are like a seed, full of wondrous potential. The environment we create should nurture the growth of each seed, and as a result, ensure the world can benefit from the fruits latent within each. The right environment relies on the quality and nature of the education that a child receives – an education that nurtures every aspect of their human identity, and encourages noble aspirations. This education, among other things, includes having the opportunity to be involved in meaningful, service-oriented community and family life, and being encouraged to reflect on and develop individual talents and qualities.
- Ruha Fifita

⁌

We can expect to spend a lot of time and energy to make incremental steps forward with our child. The efforts may or may not be cuspal. We may be doing this work without much help from others. We might make progress toward a goal that we never quite achieve. The sum of our days is not always clear.

We each have our idea of what matters—what we are supposed to do and be and what others around us are supposed to do and be. We came to those ideas through our own conditioning as we grew up. Yet, few people see the dreams for their lives turn out as they planned. Many people discover that their achievements matter little, since achievements are not the same as progress. Perhaps we see other families and think they are content, or at least they aren't as worn down as we are. We may think we are trapped. But we are not. We are free to revisit our notions of what we value and what we don't find valuable throughout our lives. We can modify our conditioning as adults and change our ideas about what matters and what we dream for the future. Our children may well be counting on us to do that.

Sometimes a big thing must happen before we revisit our ideas of what matters, especially the ideas we hold tight. Maybe divorce, death, HIV, a pandemic, or something else altogether forces us to take that second look. Such big things often happen more than once in a lifetime. Again and again, we may find ourselves examining how we grew up and came to our ideas. Through many rounds of challenge and suffering, we feel the full, terrifying impact that we are weak and mortal. In those weakest moments, we may wonder whether love can survive.

Whether literally or figuratively thrust into an emergency room, we find we are afraid. Maybe we've been injured in a traffic wreck, or our spouse has cancer, or we've both lost our jobs and must file for bankruptcy. Fear likely drives some of our first responses—especially if we believe what is unfolding could be the worst thing in our lives. When we make autism "the worst thing," we are bound to follow with certain ideas and actions. We worry that if we don't do something right away, our child won't ever talk or communicate, or won't have friends, or won't go to college, or won't get a job, or will be abandoned after we die since we aren't there to advocate and take care of them anymore.

That's one big dogpile of fear. We can revisit this notion that autism is the worst thing. We can accept that something big is happening to us and to our child as we take a second look at our ideas. We are in control of the meaning we have about what has happened. We don't have to believe that our child came into the world broken. We can decide that our child came into the world with their own strengths and weaknesses, including the strengths and weaknesses that come with their autism. Not only does that new meaning provide new views, it makes room for other ideas. That new meaning also provides us with a cushion of strength and resilience. We see where we are starting, and we start moving toward other, more powerful opportunities. The place of our child's starting point matters because we move forward from that spot. With this fresh perspective, we can examine our templates for what is good.

We also want to be part of a community that cares about our family and our child's progress. It's important to have our parents, siblings, extended family members, friends, teachers, and therapists agree on what is good and how to move toward it with us, together. Diligent professionals will be intentional and mindful about what we decide to work on. They will remember that they are getting involved in a person's life—an individual who will grow up, get a job, love someone, lose their parents, have their own dreams, and more.

In addition, good treatment means more than treatment based on the current evidence. Professionals who carve out their own small territory without looking at our whole child and family system rarely serve the greater good and for the long haul. At best, they don't contribute to our child's well-being. At worst, they become like the tail wagging the dog. Physicians at Oxford University Hospitals began to understand this problem decades ago. David Sackett and colleagues saw the emerging danger of compartmentalizing care and asked professionals to integrate a caring assessment with both wisdom and current data in their practice. Unless the decision-making includes our whole child, our whole family, and our whole cultural context, professionals risk doing their work in a self-serving, materialistic way. One piece of our child is not a billable venture. When well prepared, professionals will combine our family's wisdom with clinical evidence to make good recommendations for what is valuable and meaningful to our child.

Perhaps all this discussion of meaning and progress doesn't quite define "good." What does "good" mean for your family? We—Shahla and Peggy—don't have that answer for you and your child, but we believe you will find many answers once you commit to taking that second (or third or fourth) look and asking questions to discover what is good or at least good enough.

For Peggy, figuring out what was good and good enough proved a torturous, elusive goal when she was growing up. Her own conditioning as a child and teenager made it hard to see. What does progress look like? How does striving for continuous improvement differ from living life as if nothing is ever good enough?

When Sam landed his first job, his family and his allies agreed that sacking groceries was good enough. Peggy didn't worry that he had few ambitions with that first job. He didn't want to be a checker even though they made a lot more money. Customers could be impatient, and he might not work fast enough for them, Sam said. He didn't want to be a stocker, either. Nearly all men, the stockers worked the graveyard shift and could be raucous. Sam said that he might not work fast enough for them, either.

Yet, after he graduated with an associate's degree and certification in computer technology, he couldn't find a better job. The store had no path for loyal employees to move up. The corporate offices were on the other side of the country. Sam was underemployed and needed help with a new job search. Peggy began scouting and advocating for him again. She went back to the state agency that had worked with him to get the first job.

The agency's counselors told her that no local employer was interested in his computer skills. The counselors didn't seem to make his underemployment a priority. Many of the agency's other clients had no job at all. Peggy began to wonder whether the counselors were right: Sam had a job and it was good enough.

Two more years went by. Sam was still sacking groceries. He wasn't earning enough money to take care of himself. At this point, Sam knew the job wasn't good enough, even if the job counselors didn't agree. But he wasn't confident that he could go back to school and earn a bachelor's degree in computer science. Out of the blue, a new job counselor called with an opportunity for him. She was also surprised that the other counselors hadn't already worked with Sam to get something better.

While he would need his computer skills, the opportunity wasn't a computer job. A national grocer was opening a regional warehouse nearby. They were interested in hiring workers with disabilities. The hiring program was successful in other communities where the company had stores and warehouses.

Sam had a decision to make. He would have to quit his job sacking groceries, participate in a special, six-week training class, and then interview for the permanent, full-time job in the warehouse. Peggy wondered whether the job would be good enough, but she kept her mouth shut since Sam had a chance to quadruple his take-home pay. Maybe, like his first job, this second job was a step forward and good enough.

During the training, Sam learned many new skills and ideas, including the social and self-advocacy skills that all workers need to get hired and be considered for promotions. When the time came, he interviewed with ease and got the job on the spot. Over the next few years, he got raises and promotions. His bosses asked him to serve on the safety committee, offering another chance for him to build his social and leadership skills.

When the COVID-19 pandemic came and people shopped in panic, Sam and his coworkers had to work long, hard hours. He didn't complain, but he was candid. He and his coworkers felt as if they were barely keeping their link in the supply chain. They wondered whether they would ever catch up with the demand. Peggy thought about all the progress he'd made in the past few years. The company fostered a large, healthy space for their employees to make continuous improvement, even as the work itself seemed the same. That spirit helped Sam and his coworkers meet this new, unplanned, unprecedented, and sometimes frightening test with strength and resilience.

Peggy told Sam that he and his coworkers were heroes. When Sam was growing up, other people had called him a hero, but back then the compliment had a different meaning. He wasn't overcoming personal adversity; this time, being a hero meant something else altogether. He and his coworkers were serving the community in a time of extraordinary need.

To best see the scaffolding of what brings meaning to our lives, we can think about our actions and how (or even whether) they connect to what we value most. We may also find that as we examine our actions, we shift our values and what gives our life meaning. We can observe, evaluate, change, and revisit those ideas again and again.

Finding and making meaning follows when we respond to our child and others with dignity and humanity. Shahla's clinical work has often served families with few resources. No matter the resources, the children's teams have built constructive, reinforcing approaches so that they and their families can make progress. The teams have regularly evaluated their work and revisited their plans to remain effective and responsive to the children and their families. When programs avoided becoming a trickle-down cascade of resources, all families had a chance. Our broader society often weighs heavy on what it considers good, and those expectations could have pushed team members in different directions from what was good for an individual family. When a family is fragile, has few resources, or has values and customs that are different from the mainstream, that broad meaning of "good" may have little meaning at all. Team members had to shift over and over again as they understood, from the family members themselves, what was good or good enough for each family.

Many years ago, Shahla met three-year-old Yusuf soon after his great-aunt, Iman, received political asylum and brought Yusuf with her to the United States from a war-torn country. The team couldn't fully assess Yusuf's autism because they couldn't be sure what Yusuf understood about being in such a different environment after just a few months. In addition, he and his great-aunt were all that was left of their family. He was with her, across the street, when his parents were killed in front of them. Everything about this new life in the United States was different for Yusuf and Iman—other people's religion, skin color, food, customs, language, everything.

Iman was protective, too. She wanted Yusuf to know that the world was still a loving place despite all that had happened to them. She fed him by hand. She carried him everywhere. When she brought him to the clinic, she sat through the sessions and would not leave Yusuf alone with the others.

Some team members were shocked to see a three-year-old child still being fed like an infant. Yet, they also recognized Iman's affection and protection as she enveloped Yusuf with every kind of love that she could offer. Because Yusuf needed to work on so many things, the team decided that Iman could be the bridge to him eating more than baby mush. Rather than stop her from feeding him, they concentrated on broadening what he was eating. So, they began a program to introduce rice and lentils and other foods with taste and texture. Iman picked these items, knowing he had to eat more and different kinds of foods for his health. Iman knew she was welcome to help, stay in the room, sit in the lounge, or go out to the parking lot for some quiet time and fresh air. Together, Iman and the team decided that the goal was to successfully introduce new foods. At that moment, this was good and meaningful for her and for her beloved Yusuf.

In another case, Shahla and the team worked with a family that wanted their daughter with autism to be more active. Ana was ten years old and the middle child. Her parents and siblings were physically active, but they had little training in how to work with others to be active. As such, they weren't comfortable with a lot of structured teaching for Ana. They included Ana in most family activities, remaining gentle with her and allowing her to do whatever pleasant, appropriate activity fit the occasion. When company came over, for example, Ana might stay in the front room and line up colored beads while others watched television and talked. When they went visiting, Ana would come along, sit in a chair, and play a game on a cellphone.

The family also rode bikes together and played a little soccer. At first, with encouragement from the therapists, the family tried to include Ana on bike rides just as they included her with other family activities. That strategy didn't work. Some family members ended up riding while someone stayed home with Ana.

Ana had missed opportunities when the family was younger and activities came at a slower pace as the children learned to ride bicycles and play soccer. For this reason, it was helpful for Ana to build her skills away from the family at first. The team started a bike-riding program based on work by Michael Cameron and his colleagues. The program gently guided her through progressively more rigorous and lengthy excursions. She needed more confidence and endurance before she could have fun during riding time with family and friends. Once she had that confidence and endurance, she enjoyed being physically active, a new way of being with her friends and family.

Sometimes, we recognize that we are all learning together. Beatriz got her first period at age ten. Since the team usually worked with younger children, tackling an issue common for preteens flummoxed them. Shahla and the other therapists had their own upbringing and cultural taboos to wrestle. They lacked confidence in presenting the information that ten-year-old Beatriz and her family needed.

Expectations about sexuality, especially for young women, can vary from family to family and within and across cultures. Lucky for Beatriz, her family, and the rest of the team, renowned behavior analyst Peter Gerhardt had been in town recently. He reminded Shahla and the other therapists that their focus on younger children wasn't the only thing that made them unprepared with this matter. Behavior analysis as a young discipline and science, at least currently, casts a narrow net in its study of human behavior. Researchers are just starting to explore some of the big questions about what it means to be human. What's more, Gerhardt says, when we ask the individual with autism about what is good and meaningful, they will tell us—and we may be surprised at what they say has merit and meaning for them. Our children's dreams don't always fit what we might think.

The team realized they needed to talk with Beatriz and her family. To start, how would family members talk with any girl entering her childbearing years about relationships and sexuality? The discussion was fruitful and gave the team the language they could use to describe for Beatriz what was happening to her body as it changed and to explore her ideas and dreams. They had learned some new skills from Peter about how to approach their discussions.

Family members also said they wanted Beatriz to be able to get married one day and become a mother if that was important to her. At this point, the team went quiet. The team hadn't thought that far into the future and had made some assumptions about motherhood, especially with regard to ability and disability. Her parents had not made those assumptions because of extended family supports. Their assumption was that family values wouldn't change for Beatriz.

Beatriz's first period was a passage—the beginning of her responsibilities and choices as a woman and a milestone that prompted the team to shift directions. The team and her family began talking with Beatriz and her family about these new truths in her life and theirs. She gradually learned the words and facts that would build her agency so that she could make decisions with her family about her body, her future, and her happiness. The team's earlier notions of parenthood, especially those that seemed to require certain abilities and neurotypical ways of being, didn't fully recognize differences in all the human ways of being. There are many kinds of good mothers. The job is to grow, and to love and learn together is better. The degree of togetherness will differ across cultures.

Once we see our options, the possibilities to make meaning in our lives can be profound. In the final pages of her book, *Changed by a Child*, Barbara Gill relays how a father and his son, who could not speak, made meaning between them. The two men used a special sign language to communicate the deepest understandings that otherwise went unspoken between them. "He touches his forehead with his fingers and I touch my chest," Richard Anderson says. "I say, 'Daddy knows.'"

We can still expect a roller coaster's worth of emotions. Each parent and child approach the ride in their own way. Some embrace all the thrills ahead. Some are willing to try but won't give certain runs a second go. Some choose with care and avoid the runs with sharp drops and turns. Some may be anxious about the entire ride, but as the grandmother in the movie *Parenthood* pointed out, they may want to rethink being consigned to the merry-go-round. "That just goes around," she said. "I like the roller coaster. You get more out of it."

Our children will do things, learn things, and seek things that make us uncomfortable. They are building the scaffolding of meaning for their own life and dreaming dreams separate from us. Shahla was reminded of this when her youngest child went off to college, triggering sharp emotional turns for both of them. Her longtime friend and colleague Jamaun Willis shed light on what was happening and offered this wisdom: Don't ride their roller coaster. A behavior analyst and father of four, Willis observed that as our children grow, we no longer sit beside them in the roller coaster car. It is their ride.

For much of their childhood, we do our best to prepare. We initiate treatment, we provide bumpers, we solve problems and solve them again. Through it all, we have a compass to guide us—the love we have for our family and what we value for them. As our children reach adolescence and young adulthood, we try to shift. In most cases, we move aside so they can grow resilient and strong enough to survive the changes ahead. When our child needs long-term support, we scout again for the collaborators, advocates, and vanguards who will respect and honor our child's agency and humanity into adulthood. All of our children will do as we did when we were young: strike out on their own and make the world better than it was before, and likely in ways that we cannot foresee.

Home

Because maybe all of life is unknown and we are grappling in the dark, and at least I have the comforts that so many have not. I have family. I have warmth. I have so much love. It will be okay.
- Dara McAnulty

❧

We—Shahla and Peggy—finished writing this book as great change and challenges unfolded. The novel coronavirus and the way it spread through the United States exposed long-standing problems: a job loss can leave us without both income and health care, a beloved family member can be shot for how they look, climate change threatens horrific insecurities in our basic needs to survive. Few of us will be spared the fallout in the years ahead.

Yet, a certain grace lies within these changes, and some families, including autism families, may already recognize it: we meet life where it is. When we don't know what the future brings, the uncertainty magnifies what is meaningful and important to us in this moment.

Home is usually the place where we feel safe to think about how to develop our capacities and meet the world's challenges. At home, we decide what's good and important. We each have the capacity to figure that out in a solid, systematic way. We will likely be busy, however. There often is a lot to do.

We can work to understand more about our child, our family, and our community each day. We each have capacities and interests that direct our learning. As we make decisions about what we've learned, we seek a broader view. We start by remembering that children are born each day with capacities and interests different from those of other children and that when a child's difference diverges from the environment we've built, that difference may carry a label. Then, we remember that the science of behavior tells us how learning, progress, and happiness occur under these varied conditions. Science is on our side.

We can rally and recruit people who genuinely care about our child and our family to be by our side. If we are the parent of a two-year-old, we understand that we are responsible for almost everything in their lives. We keep their future in mind as we make decisions that ensure their choices and freedom as they grow up. If we are the parent of a fifteen-year-old, we recognize that we are becoming less responsible, so we must honor their agency and help them build skills to exercise their autonomy and their right to choose the life they wish to lead, to the degree that is possible. We remember that both parent and child are essential to professional decision-making, because our child's interests, capacities, and preferences create the possibilities. And we remain confident that there will be many moments, including difficult ones, when the people around us will show humanity at its best, from the tender gesture of a busy doctor's hand on our shoulder to the therapist who faithfully arrives on our doorstep each day at 5:30 a.m. to work with our child on toileting. We are not alone.

And we have love. Our environments—home, school, community—may be oriented toward one dominant group or another, but we can start by remembering that our covenants to one another matter. We may begin at home by changing our family's environment as we learn new skills. We might be called to make change in our community as we rally people and advocate for the changes that accommodate our child and our family. Communities create the environments that either encourage or discourage human progress. When we welcome new voices and divergent ways of being, we will also find that we are asking science to study and change our community's environments. The autism world can be a joyful, bountiful place. Our families and communities are the best place to find that bounty. Our covenants to one another must stretch to encompass well-being and meaningful living and learning for all people.

In whatever way that we find our inspiration and make meaning in our lives, we create new spaces that allow room for hope and resilience to grow. Even in the small spaces that we create with our words, new meaning can grow with language's many layers. The word "halcyon," like the word "power," entered our vocabulary and found meaning because of its storied beginnings. Human beings noted thousands of years ago that the Mediterranean Sea became calm each year around the winter solstice. Over time, people ascribed great meaning to the life-affirming change in those still waters. They told magical stories about it. Greek legend credited a bird that nested in the sea to summon the beautiful weather as a shelter for her young. Another tale said that the bird was the first eager, hopeful animal to fly from Noah's ark as the rain ended and the sun emerged. Known by two names, the halcyon and the kingfisher, this bird came to symbolize strength, nurturance, hope, and promise. Later, climatologists would turn to that ancient phenomenon and, with their scientific measurements and analytical tools, discover a recurring pattern in the jet stream that helps calm the seas. This new, scientific understanding brought yet another layer of meaning, one that is still magical in many ways. The explanations add to the inspiration, teaching us the symbolic meanings and how the world works.

Humans need both science and inspiration, it turns out. In creating new spaces both within and outside of home, we continue to connect our intellects, hearts, and souls. We understand our responsibility. We move forward. We keep learning and loving, for as we do, we build a path between now and the many possibilities for all our children.

Bibliography

The list below includes research papers, books, and other references cited in this book, along with other recommended titles for additional reading.

Ala'i-Rosales, Shahla, Samantha Cermak, and Kristin Guðmundsdóttir. 2013. "Sunny Starts: DANCE Instruction for Parents and Toddlers with ASD." In *Teaching Social Skills to People with Autism: Best Practices in Individualizing Interventions*, edited by Andy Bondy and Mary Jane Weiss. Bethesda: Woodbine House.

Ala'i-Rosales, Shahla, Joseph Cihon, Thomas Currier, Julia Ferguson, Justin Leaf, Ron Leaf, John McEachin, and Sara Weinkauf. 2018. "The Big Four: Functional Assessment Research Informs Preventative Behavior Analysis." *Behavior Analysis in Practice* 12: 222–34. https://doi.org/10.1007/s40617-018-00291-9.

Ala'i-Rosales, Shahla, and Kenda Morrison. 2019. "Barbara C. Etzel: A Conscientious Problem Solver." In *Clinical Judgment*, edited by Ron Leaf, Justin Leaf, and John McEachin. New York: Different Roads to Learning.

Ala'i-Rosales, Shahla, Karen Toussaint, and Gail McGee. 2017. "Incidental Teaching: Happy Progress." In *Handbook of Social Skills and Autism Spectrum Disorder: Assessment, Curricula, and Intervention*, edited by Justin Leaf. New York: Springer Publishing.

Ala'i-Rosales, Shahla, and Nicole Zeug. 2010. "Three Important Things to Consider When Starting Intervention for a Child Diagnosed with Autism." *Behavior Analysis in Practice* 3: 54–55. https://doi.org/10.1007/BF03391766.

Ala'i-Rosales, Shahla, Nicole Zeug, and Tanya Baynham. 2008. "The Development of Interests in Children with Autism: A Method to Establish Baselines." *Behavioral Development Bulletin* 14: 3–16. https://doi.org/10.1037/h0100502.

Baer, Donald, and James Sherman. 1964. "Reinforcement Control of Generalized Imitation in Young Children." *Journal of Experimental Child Psychology* 1: 37–49.

Baer, Donald, and Montrose Wolf. 1967. "The Entry into Natural Communities of Reinforcement." Paper presented at the Achieving Generality of Behavioral Change Symposium, American Psychological Association, Washington, D.C.

Bannerman, Diane, Jan Sheldon, James Sherman, and Alan Harchik. 1990. "Balancing the Right to Habilitation with the Right to Personal Liberties: The Rights of People with Developmental Disabilities to Eat Too Many Doughnuts and Take a Nap." *Journal of Applied Behavior Analysis* 23(1): 79–89. https://doi.org/10.1901/jaba.1990.23-79.

Barahona, Heather. 2010. "A Training Program to Facilitate Caregiver Involvement in School Meetings." Master's thesis, University of North Texas. https://digital.library.unt.edu/ark:/67531/metadc30434/.

Barrera, Isaura, and Lucinda Kramer. 2009. *Using Skilled Dialogue to Transform Challenging Interactions: Honoring Identity, Voice and Connection*. Baltimore: Brookes Publishing.

Bauman, Margaret, and Thomas L. Kemper. 1985. "Histoanatomic observations of the brain in early infantile autism." *Neurology* 35(6): 866. https://doi.org/10.1212/wnl.35.6.866.

Benner, Patricia. 2004. "Using the Dreyfus Model of Skill Acquisition to Describe and Interpret Skill Acquisition and Clinical Judgement." *Bulletin of Science, Technology and Society* 24: 188–99. https://doi.org/10.1177/0270467604265061.

Bernal, Martha. 1972. "Behavioral Treatment of a Child's Eating Problem." *Journal of Behavior Therapy and Experimental Psychology* 3(1): 43–50. https://doi.org/10.1016/0005-7916(72)90032-8.

Biglan, Anthony, Brian Flay, Dennis Embry, and Irwin Sandler. 2012. "The Critical Role of Nurturing Environments for Promoting Human Well-Being." *Journal of Abnormal and Social Psychology* 67(4): 257–71. https://doi.org/10.1037/a0026796.

Biglan, Tony. 2015. *The Nurture Effect: How the Science of Human Behavior Can Improve Our Lives and Our World*. Oakland: New Harbinger Publications.

Binder, Carl. 1996. "Behavioral Fluency: Evolution of a New Paradigm." *The Behavior Analyst* 19: 163–97. https://doi.org/10.1007/BF03393163.

Binder, Carl. 2016. "Integrating Organizational-Cultural Values with Performance Management." *Journal of Organizational Behavior Management*, 36(2-3): 185-201. https://doi.org/10.1080/01608061.2016.1200512

Black, Edwin. 2003. *War Against the Weak: Eugenics and America's Campaign to Create a Master Race*. New York: Four Walls Eight Windows.

Bondy, Andy, and Lori Frost. 1994. "The Picture Exchange Communication System." *Focus on Autistic Behavior* 9(3): 1–19. https://doi.org/10.1177/108835769400900301.

Brown, Lou, Mary Beth Branston-McClean, Diane Baumgart, Lisbeth Vincent, Mary Falvey, and Jack Schroeder. 1979. "Using the Characteristics of Current and Subsequent Least Restrictive Environments in the Development of Curricular Content for Severely Handicapped Students." *Research and*

Practice for Persons with Severe Disabilities 4(4): 407–24. https://doi.org/10.1177/154079697900400408.

Callahan, Kevin, and Joyce Rademacher. 1999. "Use of Self-Management Strategies to Increase the On-Task Behavior of a Student with Autism." *Journal of Positive Behavior Interventions* 1(2): 117–22. https://doi.org/10.1177/109830079900100206.

Cameron Michael, Robert Shapiro, and Susan Ainsleigh. 2005. "Bicycle Riding: Pedaling Made Possible Through Positive Behavioral Interventions." *Journal of Positive Behavior Interventions* 7(3): 153–58. https://doi.org/10.1177/10983007050070030401.

Carr, Edward. 1977. "The Motivation of Self-Injurious Behavior: A Review of Some Hypotheses." *Psychological Bulletin* 54: 800–16. https://doi.org/10.1037/0033-2909.84.4.800.

Celiberti, David. 2015. "An Interview with Catherine Maurice, PhD, Parent, Author, and Founding Board Member of the Association for Science in Autism Treatment." *Science in Autism Treatment* 12(4): 3–17.

Celiberti, David, and Sandra Harris. 1993. "Behavioral Intervention for Siblings of Children with Autism: A Focus on Skills to Enhance Play." *Behavior Therapy* 24(4): 573–99. https://doi.org/10.1016/S0005-7894(05)80319-3.

Charlop, Marjorie, Patricia Kurtz, and Fran Casey. 1990. "Using Aberrant Behaviors as Reinforcers for Autistic Children." *Journal of Applied Behavior Analysis* 23(2): 163–81. https://doi.org/10.1901/jaba.1990.23-163.

Cihon, Joseph. 2015. "Yummy Starts: A Constructional Approach to Food Selectivity with Children with Autism." Master's thesis, University of North Texas. https://digital.library.unt.edu/ark:/67531/metadc799526/.

Cihon, Traci, Joseph Cihon, and Guy Bedient. 2016. "Establishing a Common Vocabulary of Key Concepts for the Effective Implementation of Applied Behavior Analysis." *International Electronic Journal of Elementary Education (Special Issue)* 9(2): 337-348.

Czekalski, Sara. 2009. "What You Teach Makes A Difference: Direct and Collateral Outcomes of an Autism Sibling Intervention." Master's thesis, University of North Texas. https://digital.library.unt.edu/ark:/67531/metadc10996/.

Dalai Lama, The, and Desmond Tutu with Douglas Abrams. 2016. *The Book of Joy*. New York: Avery.

Donvan, John, and Caren Zucker. 2016. *In a Different Key: A History of Autism*. New York: Crown Publishing Group.

Ducharme, Joseph, and David Worling. 1994. "Behavioral Momentum and Stimulus Fading in the Acquisition and Maintenance of Child Compliance in the Home." *Journal of Applied Behavior Analysis* 27: 639–47. https://doi.org/10.1901/jaba.1994.27-639.

Dunlap, Glenn, Edward Carr, Robert Horner, Jennifer Zarcone, and Ilene Schwartz. 2008. "Positive Behavior Support and Applied Behavior Analysis: A Familial Alliance." *Behavior Modification* 32: 682–98. https://doi.org/10.1177/0145445508317132.

Dunlap, Glenn, and Frank Robbins. 1991. "Current Perspectives in Service Delivery for Young Children with Autism." *Comprehensive Mental Health Care* 1: 177–94.

Dunst, Carl, and Carol Trivette. 2012. "Moderators of the Effectiveness of Adult Learning Method Practices." *Journal of Social Sciences* 8(2): 143–48. https://doi.org/10.3844/jssp.2012.143.148.

Dunst, Carl, Carol Trivette, and Deborah Hamby. 2007. "Meta-Analysis of Family-Centered Helpgiving Practices Research." *Special issue: Families of Children with Developmental Disabilities* 13: 370–78. https://doi.org/10.1002/mrdd.20176.

Ellis, Ellyn, Shahla Ala'i-Rosales, Sigrid Glenn, Jesus Rosales-Ruiz, and Joel Greenspoon. 2006. "The Effects of Graduated Exposure, Modeling, and Contingent Social Attention on Tolerance to Skin Care Products with Two Children with Autism." *Research in Developmental Disabilities* 27: 585–98.

Ennis-Cole, Demetria. 2019. *Seeing Autism Through Parents' Feedback, Sketchnotes, Technology, and Evidence-Based Practice.* New York: Springer Publishing.

Etzel, Barbara, and Judith LeBlanc. 1979. "The Simplest Treatment Alternative: The Law of Parsimony Applied to Choosing Appropriate Instructional Control and Errorless-Learning Procedures for the Difficult-To-Teach Child." *Journal of Autism and Developmental Disorders* 9(4): 361–82. https://doi.org/10.1007/BF01531445.

Fawcett, Stephen. 1991. "Some Values Guiding Community Research." *Journal of Applied Behavior Analysis* 24: 621–36. https://doi.org/10.1901/jaba.1991.24-621.

Frey, Jennifer, and Ann Kaiser. 2010. "The Use of Play Expansions to Increase the Diversity and Complexity of Object Play in Young Children with Disabilities." *Topics in Early Childhood Education* 31: 99–111. https://doi.org/10.1177/0271121410378758.

Garden, Regan. 2016. "Creating a Verbal Community for Describing Emotional Responses within a Contingency Lens: The Effects of a Brief Training Workshop." Master's thesis, University of North Texas. https://digital.library.unt.edu/ark:/67531/metadc955041.

Gena, Angeliki, Petros Galanis, Shahla Ala'i-Rosales, and Eleni Michalopoulou. 2013. "Systemic Behavior Analytic Applications for the Treatment of Children with ASD: Pilot Results Depicting Naturalistic Parent-Child Interaction." Proceedings of the World Psychiatric Association Thematic Conference on Intersectional Collaboration, Greece. https://bit.ly/351rSwX.

Gena, Angeliki, Petros Galanis, and Erifylli Tsirempolou. 2016. "Parent Training for Families with a Child with ASD: A Naturalistic Systemic Behavior Analytic Model." *The European Journal of Counselling Psychology* 4: 4–31. https://doi.org/10.5964/ejcop.v4i1.72.

Gerhardt, Peter. 2019. "Sexuality, Autism, and the Behavior Analyst." Interview by *The Daily BA*. July 3. https://www.youtube.com/watch?v=UKmNlZ0tcYk.

Gerhardt, Peter. 2020. *Social Skills and Adaptive Behavior in Learners with Autism Spectrum Disorder*. Baltimore: Paul H. Brookes Publishing Co.

Gill, Barbara. 1998. *Changed by a Child: Companion Notes for Parents of a Child with a Disability*. New York: Harmony Books.

Goldiamond, Israel. 1974. "Toward a Constructional Approach to Social Problems: Ethical and Constitutional Issues Raised by Applied Behavior Analysis." *Behavior and Social Issues* 11: 108–97. https://doi.org/10.5210/bsi.v11i2.92.

Goldiamond, Israel. 1975. "A Construction Approach to Self-Control." In *Social Casework: A Behavioral Approach*, edited by Arthur Schwartz and Israel Goldiamond. New York: Columbia University.

Goldstein, Howard, Louise Kaczmarek, and Nancy Hepting. 1996. "Indicators of Quality in Communication Intervention." In *Early Intervention/Early Childhood Special Education: Recommended Practices*, edited by Samuel Odom and Mary McLean. Austin: Pro-Ed.

Grandin, Temple. 2006. *Thinking in Pictures: My Life with Autism*. New York: Vintage Books.

Grandin, Temple, and Margaret Scariano. 1986. *Emergence: Labeled Autistic*. New York: Warner Books.

Green, Carolyn, and Dennis Reid. 1999. "Reducing Indices of Unhappiness Among Individuals with Profound Multiple Disabilities During Therapeutic Exercise Routines." *Journal of Applied Behavior Analysis* 32(2): 137–47. https://doi.org/10.1901/jaba.1999.32-137.

Guðmundsdóttir, Kristin, Shahla Ala'i-Rosales, and Zuilma Sigurðardóttir. 2018. "Extending Caregiver Training via Telecommunication for Rural Children with Autism." *Rural Special Education Quarterly* 38(1): 26–42. https://doi.org/10.1177/8756870518783522.

Gustaferro, Kaitlyn, and John Lutzker. 2018. *A Guide to Programs for Parenting Children with Autism Spectrum Disorder, Intellectual Disabilities or Developmental Disabilities: Evidence-Based Guidance for Professionals*. London: Jessica Kingsley Publishers.

Harchik, Alan, James Sherman, Jan Sheldon, and Diane Bannerman, 1993. "Choice and Control: New Opportunities for People with Disabilities." *Annals of Clinical Psychiatry* 5: 151–63.

Harris, Sandra, and Beth Glasberg. 2003. *Siblings of Children with Autism: A Guide for Families.* Bethesda: Woodbine House.
Heinkel-Wolfe, Peggy. 2008. *See Sam Run: A Mother's Memoir of Autism.* Denton, Texas: University of North Texas Press.
Higashida, Naoki. 2016. *The Reason I Jump: The Inner Voice of a Thirteen-Year-Old Boy with Autism.* New York: Random House.
Hiltz, Philip. 1962. *Behavior Mod.* New York: Bantam Books.
Hineline, Philip, and Jesus Rosales-Ruiz. 2013. "Behavior in Relation to Aversive Events: Punishment and Negative Reinforcement." In *APA Handbook of Behavior Analysis, Vol. 1., Methods and Principles*, edited by Gregory Madden. Washington, D.C.: American Psychological Association.
Horner, Robert, Edward Carr, James Halle, Gail McGee, Samuel Odom, and Mark Wolery. 2005. "The Use of Single-Subject Research to Identify Evidence-Based Practice." *Exceptional Children* 71: 165–79. https://doi.org/10.1177/001440290507100203.
Howard, Jane, Coleen Sparkman, Howard Cohen, Gina Green, and Harold Stanislaw. 2005. "A Comparison of Behavior Analytic and Eclectic Early Interventions for Young Children with Autism." *Research in Developmental Disabilities* 26: 359–83. https://doi.org/10.1016/j.ridd.2004.09.005.
Howard, Jane, Harold Stanislaw, Gina Green, Coleen Sparkman, and Howard Cohen. 2014. "Comparison of Behavior Analytic and Eclectic Early Interventions for Young Children with Autism After Three Years." *Research in Developmental Disabilities* 35: 3326–44. http://dx.doi.org/10.1016/j.ridd.2014.08.021.
Kaiser, Ann, and Megan Roberts. 2011. "Advances in Early Communication and Language Intervention." *Journal of Early Intervention* 33: 298–309. https://doi.org/10.1177/1053815111429968.
Kaiser, Ann, Terry Hancock, and Jennifer Nietfeld. 2000. "The Effects of Parent-Implemented Enhanced Milieu Teaching on the Social Communication of Children Who Have Autism." *Early Education and Development* 11(4): 423-446. https://doi.org/10.1207/s15566935eed1104_4.
Karasik, Paul, and Judy Karasik. 2010. *The Ride Together: A Brother and Sister's Memoir of Autism in the Family.* New York: Simon and Schuster (Washington Square Press).
Keenan, Mickey, Karola Dillenburger, Paolo Moderato, and Hanns-Rüdiger Röttgers. 2010. "Science for Sale in a Free Market Economy: But at What Price? ABA and the Treatment of Autism in Europe." *Behavior and Social Issues* 19: 126–43. https://doi.org/10.5210/bsi.v19i0.2879.
Kelly, Amy and Matt Tinacani. 2013. "Collaborative Training and Practice Among Applied Behavior Analysts Who Support Individuals with Autism Spectrum

Disorder." *Education and Training in Autism and Developmental Disabilities* 48: 120–31.

Klintwall, Lars, and Svein Eikeseth. 2014. "Early and Intensive Intervention in Autism." In *Comprehensive Guide to Autism*, edited by Vinood Patel. New York: Springer Publishing. https://doi.org/10.1007/978-1-4614-4788-7_129.

Koegel, Lynn, Kristen Ashbaugh, Anahita Navab, and Robert Koegel. 2016. "Improving Empathic Communication Skills in Adults with Autism Spectrum Disorder." *Journal of Autism and Developmental Disorders* 46(3): 921–33. https://doi.org/10.1007/s10803-015-2633-0.

Koegel, Lynn, Robert Koegel, Christine Hurley, and William Frea. 1992. "Improving Social Skills and Disruptive Behavior in Children with Autism through Self-Management." *Journal of Applied Behavior Analysis*,25(2): 341–53. https://doi.org/10.1901/jaba.1992.25-341.

Koegel, Lynn, and Claire LaZebnik. 2014. *Overcoming Autism: Finding the Answers, Strategies, and Hope That Can Transform a Child's Life*. New York: Penguin Books.

Koegel, Lynn, Robert Koegel, William Frea, and Israel Green-Hopkins. 2003. "Priming as a Method of Coordinating Educational Services for Students with Autism." *Language, Speech, and Hearing Services in Schools*, 34(3): 228-235. https://doi.org/10.1044/0161-1461(2003/19)

Koegel, Robert, Daniel Openden, and Lynn Koegel. 2004. "A Systematic Desensitization Paradigm to Treat Hypersensitivity to Auditory Stimuli in Children with Autism in Family Contexts." *Research and Practice for Persons with Severe Disabilities* 29(2): 122–34. https://doi.org/10.2511/rpsd.29.2.122.

Koegel, Robert, Ty Vernon, and Lynn Koegel. 2009. "Improving Social Initiations in Young Children with Autism Using Reinforcers with Embedded Social Interactions." *Journal of Autism and Developmental Disorders* 39(9): 1240–51. https://doi.org/10.1007/s10803-009-0732-5.

Kohr, Melinda, John Parrish, Nancy Neef, Joan Driessen, and Patrician Hallinan. 1988. "Communication Skills Training for Parents: Experimental and Social Validation." *Journal of Applied Behavior Analysis* 21: 21–30. https://doi/abs/10.1901/jaba.1988.21-21.

Kubina, Richard, and Kirsten Yurich. 2009. "Developing Behavioral Fluency for Students with Autism: A Guide for Parents and Teachers." *Intervention in School and Clinic* 44: 131–38. https://doi.org/10.1177/1053451208326054.

LaFrance, Danielle, Mary Jane Weiss, Ellie Kazemi, Joanne Gerenser, and Jacqueline Dobres. 2019. "Multidisciplinary Teaming: Enhancing Collaboration Through Increased Understanding." *Behavior Analysis in Practice* 12: 709–26. https://doi.org/10.1007/s40617-019-00331-y.

Latham, Glenn. 1994. *Power of Positive Parenting: A Wonderful Way to Raise Children*. North Logan: P & T Ink.

Latham, Glenn. 2015. *An Angel Out of Tune*. Audiobook. North Logan: P & T Ink.

Layng, T.V. Joe. 2017. "Private Emotions as Contingency Descriptors: Emotions, Emotional Behavior, and Their Evolution." *European Journal of Behavior Analysis* 18(2): 168–79. https://doi.org/10.1080/15021149.2017.1304875.

Leaf, Justin, Joseph Cihon, Ron Leaf, John McEachin, and Mitchell Taubman. 2016. "A Progressive Approach to Discrete Trial Teaching." *International Electronic Journal of Elementary Education* 9: 361–72.

Leaf, Justin, Ron Leaf, Mitchell Taubman, John McEachin, Shahla Ala'i-Rosales, Robert Ross, Tristram Smith, and Mary Jane Weiss. 2015. "Applied Behavior Analysis is a Science and, Therefore, Progressive." *Journal of Autism and Developmental Disorders* 46: 720–31. https://doi.org/10.1007/s10803-015-2591-6

Leaf, Ron, John McEachin, and Jaisom Harsh. 1999. *A Work In Progress: Behavior Management Strategies and a Curriculum for Intensive Behavioral Treatment of Autism*. New York: DRL Books.

Leaf, Ron, Mitchell Taubman, John McEachin, Justin Leaf, and Kathleen Tsuji. 2011. "A Program Description of a Community-Based Intensive Behavioral Intervention Program for Individuals with Autism Spectrum Disorders." *Education and Treatment of Children* 34: 259–85.

LeBlanc, Linda, Tyra Sellers, and Shahla Ala'i. 2020. *Building and Sustaining Meaningful and Effective Relationships as a Supervisor and Mentor*. New York: Sloan Publishing.

Lindsley, Ogden R. 1964. "Direct Measurement and Prosthesis of Retarded Behavior." *Journal of Education* 147(1): 62–81. https://doi.org/10.1177/002205746414700107.

Louis, Donald, and Rosalva Resendiz. 1997. "Sensitizing Officers to Persons with Developmental Disabilities. A Curriculum Guide for Law Enforcement Trainers." Denton, Texas: University of North Texas. ERIC Document Reproduction Service No. ED408503.

Lovaas, O. Ivar. 1987. "Behavioral Treatment and Normal Educational and Intellectual Functioning in Young Autistic Children." *Journal of Consulting and Clinical Psychology* 55: 3–9. https://doi.org/10.1037//0022-006x.55.1.3.

Lovaas, O. Ivar, Robert Koegel, James Simmons, and Judith Long. 1973. "Some Generalization and Follow-Up Measures on Autistic Children in Behavior Therapy." *Journal of Applied Behavior Analysis* 6: 131–65. https://doi.org/10.1901/jaba.1973.6-131.

Lutzker, John, and Randy Campbell. 1994. *Ecobehavioral Family Interventions in Developmental Disabilities*. Pacific Grove, Calif.: Brooks/Cole Publishing Company.

Magito McLaughlin, Darlene, and Edward Carr. 2005. "Quality of Rapport as a Setting Event for Problem Behavior: Assessment and Intervention." *Journal of Positive Behavior Interventions* 7(2): 68–91. https://doi.org/10.1177/10983007050070020401.

Marcus, Adam. 2020. "Journal Flags—But Does Not Retract—Decades-Old Paper on 'Correcting' Gender Identity." *Retraction Watch*, Oct. 22. https://retractionwatch.com/2020/10/22/journal-flags-but-does-not-retract-decades-old-paper-on-correcting-gender-identity.

Maurice, Catherine. 1994. *Let Me Hear Your Voice: A Family's Triumph Over Autism.* New York: Ballantine Books.

McAnulty, Dara. 2020. *Diary of a Young Naturalist.* Dorset: Little Toller.

McClannahan, Lynn, and Patricia Krantz. 1999. *Topics in Autism. Activity Schedules for Children with Autism: Teaching Independent Behavior.* Bethesda: Woodbine House.

McClannahan, Lynn, Gail McGee, Gregory MacDuff, and Patricia Krantz. 1990. "Assessing and Improving Child Care: A Personal Appearance Index for Children with Autism." *Journal of Applied Behavior Analysis* 23(4): 469–82. https://doi.org/10.1901/jaba.1990.23-469.

McGee, Gail, Connie Almeida, Beth Sulzer-Azaroff, and Robert Feldman. 1992. "Promoting Reciprocal Interactions Via Peer Incidental Teaching." *Journal of Applied Behavior Analysis* 25(1): 117–126. https://doi.org/10.1901/jaba.1992.25-117.

McGee, Gail, Michael Morrier, and Shahla Ala'i-Rosales. 2019. "Contributions of University Lab Schools to Behavior Analysis." *European Journal of Behavior Analysis* 21(1): 74–91. https://doi.org/10.1080/15021149.2019.1616988.

Miller, Kristin, Alicia Re Cruz, and Shahla Ala'i-Rosales. 2019. "Inherent Tensions and Possibilities: Behavior Analysis and Cultural Responsiveness." *Behavior and Social Issues* 28: 16–36. https://doi.org/10.1007/s42822-019-00010-1.

Odom, Samuel. 2009. "The Tie That Binds: Evidence-Based Practice, Implementation Science and Outcomes for Children." *Topics in Early Childhood Special Education* 29(1): 53–61. https://doi.org/10.1177/0271121408329171.

Odom, Samuel, Mary McLean, Lawrence Johnson, and Margaret LaMontagne. 1995. "Recommended Practices in Early Childhood Special Education: Validation and Current Use." *Journal of Early Intervention* 19: 1–17. https://doi.org/10.1177/105381519501900101.

Orso, Anna. 2020. "Philadelphia Was Told to Brace for Mass Unrest After the Election. Instead, the City Danced. *The Philadelphia Inquirer*, Nov. 9, 2020. https://www.inquirer.com/news/philadelphia/philadelphia-election-dance-party-philly-elmo-biden-trump-working-families-party-20201109.html

Owens, Dierdre Cooper. 2018. *Medical Bondage: Race, Gender and the Origins of American Gynecology*. Athens, Ga.: University of Georgia Press.

Park, Clara. 1968 (reissue 1982). *The Siege: A Family's Journey into the World of an Autistic Child*. New York: Back Bay Books.

Parsons, Marsha, Jeannia Rollyson, and Dennis Reid. 2012. "Evidence-Based Staff Training: A Guide for Practitioners." *Behavior Analysis in Practice* 5: 2–12. https://doi.org/10.1007/BF03391819.

Prevedini, Anna, Tatja Hirvikoski, Tiina Holmberg Bergman, Bella Berg, Giovanni Miselli, Francesca Pergolizzi, and Paolo Moderato. 2020. "ACT-based Interventions for Reducing Psychological Distress in Parents and Caregivers of Children with Autism Spectrum Disorders: Recommendations for Higher Education Programs." *European Journal of Behavior Analysis* 21: 133–57. https://doi.org/10.1080/15021149.2020.1729023.

Pritchett, Malika, Shahla Ala'i, Alicia Re Cruz, and Traci Cihon. 2021. "Social Justice is the Spirit and Aim of an Applied Science of Human Behavior: An Examination and Reflection of the Variables Related to Moving From Colonial to Participatory Research." *Behavior Analysis in Practice*. https://doi.org/10.31234/osf.io/t87p4.

Risley, Todd. 1996. "Get a Life!" In *Positive Behavioral Supports: Including People with Difficult Behavior in the Community*, edited by Lynn Koegel, Robert Koegel, and Glenn Dunlap. Baltimore: P.H. Brookes.

Rolfe, Randall Colton. 1990. *You Can Postpone Anything But Love: Expanding our Potential as Parents*. New York: Warner Books.

Rosales-Ruiz, Jesus. 2003. "D. M. Baer Developmental Psychology: Why Wait? Shape It!" In *A Small Matter of Proof: The Legacy of Donald M. Baer*, edited by Karen Budd and Trevor Stokes. Reno: Context Press.

Rosales-Ruiz, Jesus, and Don Baer. 1997. "Behavioral Cusps: A Developmental and Pragmatic Concept for Behavior Analysis." *Journal of Applied Behavior Analysis* 30: 533–44. https://doi.org/10.1901/jaba.

Rosenberg, Nancy, and Ilene Schwartz. 2018. "Guidance or Compliance: What Makes an Ethical Behavior Analyst?" *Behavior Analysis in Practice* 12(4). https://doi.org/10.1007/s40617-018-00287-5.

Sackett, David, William Rosenberg, Muir Gray, Bryan Haynes, and Scott Richardson. 1996. "Evidence Based Medicine: What It Is and What It Isn't." *British Medical Journal* 312(7023): 71–72. https://doi.org/10.1136/bmj.312.7023.71.

Schneider, Susan. 2012. *The Science of Consequences: How They Affect Genes, Change the Brain and Impact our World*. New York: Prometheus Books.

Schriebman, Laura, Geraldine Dawson, Aubyn Stahmer, Rebecca Landa, Sally Rogers, Gail McGee, Connie Kasari, Brooke Ingersoll, Ann Kaiser,

Yvonne Bruinsma, Erin McNerney, Amy Wetherby, and Alycia Halladay. 2015. "Naturalistic Developmental Behavioral Interventions. Empirically Validated Treatments for Autism Spectrum Disorder." *Journal of Autism and Developmental Disorders* 45(8): 2411–28. https://doi.org/10.1007/s10803-015-2407-8.

Schwartz, Ilene, and Elizabeth Kelly. 2021. "Quality of Life for People with Disabilities: Why Applied Behavior Analysts Should Consider This a Primary Dependent Variable." *Research and Practice for Persons with Severe Disabilities*. In publication. https://doi.org/10.1177/15407969211033629.

Sellers, Tyra, Shahla Ala'i-Rosales, and Rebecca McDonald, R. 2016. "Taking Full Responsibility: The Ethics of Supervision in Behavior Analytic Practice." *Behavior Analysis in Practice* 9: 299–308. https://doi.org/10.1007/s40617-016-0144-x.

Sherman, J. A. 1971. "Imitation and Language Development." In *Advances in Child Development and Behavior*, edited by Hayne Reese and Lewis Lipsitt. New York: Academic Press.

Skinner, B. F. 1978. "The Ethics of Helping People." In *Reflections on Behaviorism and Society*. Englewood Cliffs, N.J.: Prentice-Hall.

Slocum, Timothy, Ronnie Detrich, Susan Wilczynski, Trina Spencer, Teri Lewis, and Katie Wolfe. 2015. "The Evidence-Based Practice of Applied Behavior Analysis." *The Behavior Analyst* 37: 41–56. https://doi.org/10.1007/s40614-014-0005-2.

Solomon, Andrew. 2013. *Far From the Tree: Parents, Children and the Search for Identity*. New York: Scribner Books.

Smith, Garnett, Dennis McDougall, and Patricia Edelen-Smith. 2006. "Behavioral Cusps: A Person-Centered Concept for Establishing Pivotal Individual, Family, and Community Behaviors and Repertoires." *Focus on Autism and Other Developmental Disabilities* 21(4): 223–29. https://doi.org/10.1177/10883576060210040301.

Smith, Tristram. 2001. "Discrete Trial Training in the Treatment of Autism." *Focus on Autism and Other Developmental Disabilities* 16: 86–92. https://doi.org/10.1177/108835760101600204.

Sugai, George, Breda O'Keeffe, and Lindsay Fallon. 2012. "A Contextual Consideration of Culture and School-Wide Positive Behavior Support." *Journal of Positive Behavior Interventions* 14: 197–208. https://doi.org/10.1177/1098300711426334.

Tsouderos, Trine, and Patricia Callahan. 2009. "Risky Alternative Therapies Have Little Basis in Science." *Chicago Tribune,* Nov. 22, 2009. (Comments retrieved Dec. 2009). https://www.chicagotribune.com/lifestyles/health/chi-autism-treatments-nov22-story.html.

United Nations General Assembly, U.N. Commission on Human Rights. 1959. *Declaration of the Rights of the Child, Resolution 1386/14.*

Valle, Jan. 2018. "Across the Conference Table: Private and Public Mothering of Children with Learning Disabilities." *Learning Disability Quarterly* 41(1): 7–18. https://doi.org/10.1177/0731948717696258.

Vandercook, Terri, Jennifer York, and Marsha Forest. 1989. "The McGill Action Planning System (MAPS): A Strategy for Building the Vision." *The Journal of the Association for Persons with Severe Handicaps* 14: 205–15. https://doi.org/10.1177/154079698901400306.

Weinkauf, Sara, Nicole Zeug, Claire Anderson, and Shahla Ala'i-Rosales. 2011. "Evaluating the Effectiveness of a Comprehensive Staff Training Package for Behavioral Interventions for Children With Autism." *Research in Autism Spectrum Disorders* 5: 864–71. https://doi.org/10.1016/j.rasd.2010.10.001

Wenger, Etienne, Richard McDermott, and William Snyder. 2002. *Cultivating Communities of Practice: A Guide to Managing Knowledge.* Boston: Harvard Business School Press.

Wolf, Montrose. 1978. "Social Validity: The Case for Subjective Measurement or How Applied Behavior Analysis is Finding its Heart." *Journal of Applied Behavior Analysis* 11(2): 203–214. https://doi.org/10. 1901/jaba.1978.11-203.

Wolf, Montrose, Todd Risley, and Hayden Mees. 1964. "Application of Operant Conditioning Procedures to the Behaviour Problems of an Autistic Child." *Behavior Research and Therapy* 1: 305–12.

Acknowledgements

Shahla thanks all the children, parents, families, and students who have blessed her journey. Special thanks to her early teachers, Juliette Whittaker, Marla Muxen, John and Sandra Lutzker, Jan Sheldon, James Sherman, Ogden Lindsley, Barbara Etzel, Kenda Morrison, Michael Fabrizio, and Jesus Rosales-Ruiz. Each taught her to orient to the North Star of science and compassion.

Peggy thanks fellow participants of the 2015 Santa Fe Science Writing Workshop, particularly the workshop leaders, Sandra Blakeslee and George Johnson, who shared their wisdom in finding and sharing science's big ideas for everyday readers.

We both thank Paige Wolfe for many hours reviewing and editing early versions of this book's manuscript and Ashleigh Imus for her editorial insights that brought clarity to the final draft. We also thank dear friends Jessica Broome, Kenda Morrison, and Demetria Ennis-Cole, who read early drafts and gave feedback and support. And we thank Ron Leaf for his enthusiasm and for introducing us to the crew at Different Roads to Learning, who recognized the value of this work and gave it life.

Finally, we thank our families, without whose support and encouragement this book—a decade in the making—would never have come to pass.

Index

Abdul-Baha, 112
Acceptance and Commitment Therapy (ACT), 120
acceptance of others, 125
adaptive strategies/skills, 131, 133
adolescence, 107, 127–28, 132, 148
adults with autism
    early adulthood, 107, 117, 148
    harms experienced as children, 11
    new boundaries and roles in, 98
    perspectives of, 117
    push back against developments in field, 11
    services for, 107
advancements in societal attitudes toward autism, 10
adversity, learning to tolerate, 134
advocacy groups, 96
advocacy role of parents/caregivers, 97
affection, showing, 135. See also love and loving
agency of children with autism, 78–81, 147
aggressive behaviors, 132
alliances, 108–9
alterations to treatments, 41
Anderson, Richard, 147
Angelou, Maya, 73
An Angel Out Of Tune (Latham), 42
anger, 55, 56
antecedent stimuli, 29
anti-authority attitudes, 53, 54
applied behavior analysis, 20, 21, 22, 24–25
Applied Behavior Analysis International, 102
art and literature, 135
assessments, 40

Association of Professional Behavior Analysts, 102
attention
    to child's bids for connection, 139–40
    connections made with shared, 138
    and development of communication skills, 131
    as reinforcing behavior, 31
    self-monitoring of, 34
    struggling for, 131–32
    value of full and focused, 128–34
attitudes/perspectives, importance of, 52–55, 84–87
audiologists, 101–2, 104
autism
    label, 9–10
    term usage in book, 19
aversive behavioral techniques, 67–68, 123

Baer, Donald, 60
Baker, Mary, 75, 136–37
Baldwin, James A., 101
Ball, Michael, 75
Barahona, Heather, 96–97
basic care, provision of, 126
Baum, L. Frank, 9, 12
behavior, human, 29–30
behavioral cusps, 60–64, 65, 67, 77
behavioral problems, 130–31
behavioral science
    aversive techniques, 67–68, 123
    behavior analysts' expertise with, 71
    and clinical practice, 28
    constructional approach of, 28
    language of, 29–30
    progress inherent in, 28
    shaping (technique), 137–39
    study of reinforcement, 31

See also interventions, behavioral
behavior analysis/analysts
    and Acceptance and Commitment Therapy, 120
    alterations/substitutions made by, 41
    and assessments, 40
    and behavioral science, 71
    contingencies developed by, 30
    continuous improvement of, 41
    early research on autism, 24–26
    encouraging independence of children, 81
    expertise of professionals, 36, 37–39, 44–45, 71
    external prompts used by, 40
    history of, 18
    inexperienced/unskilled, 39–42, 137–38
    and intentions underlying treatments, 92–94
    and learning environments, 40
    mentors of, 39
    and preferences of children, 70–71
    as product of experimental psychology, 18, 21
    professional standards/credentials, 27, 41, 102
    responsiveness to children, 41
    and science of behavior change, 35–36, 42
    and understanding of human behavior, 146
    and understanding of learning, 20
    and values/cultures of families, 81
Behavior Analysis Certification Board, 102
Bernal, Martha, 66
biological origins of autism, 115
blind spots, seeing around, 84–87
bodily products, disgust in response to, 126–27
body odors, 127–28
Bondy, Andy, 131
bookmark identifying topics of discussions for parents, 96–97
books as sources of connection, 108
Buddha, 17

businesses serving autism community, 26–28, 49
Callahan, Kevin, 34
Cameron, Michael, 146
Campbell, Randy, 86, 98–99, 100, 122
Cascio, Jamais, 43
Celiberti, David, 100
centers for autism treatment, 57–58
change
    difficulties with, 133
    intentional, 57–64
Changed by a Child (Gill), 147
Charlop, Marjorie, 45, 71
checklists, 17–18
chelation therapy, 53–54
Chicago Tribune, 53–54
child abuse/neglect, 100–101
Cihon, Joe, 66
cleanliness, expectations of, 126–27
clinical trials, 103
clothing, learning goals related to, 51–52
coercion, 40
collaboration, 84
communication skills
    adopting alternative forms of, 123
    and early interventions, 123
    importance of, 32
    and joyful interactions, 113
    nurturing, 131
    responding to struggles with, 130
    of Sam, 59–60, 89, 130, 131
communities, 95–96, 124, 150
compartmentalizing care, dangers of, 142
complex situations faced by parents, 18
compliance and agency, 79
comprehensive treatment programs, 48–49

computer games, 133
connecting and connections, 73–109
    attending to bids for, 139–40
    being and equal among professionals, 87–91
    building resilience and strength, 78–81
    and eye-contact difficulties, 129
    within families, 74–78, 98–101, 119, 124, 139–40
    and feelings of disgust, 127
    and focused attention, 129
    fostered by routines, 119
    with intention, 108–9
    learning from one another, 82–84
    made with shared attention, 138
    nurturing, 131, 137
    power of, 13–14
    and professional standards/credentials, 101–4
    reciprocity as means of fostering, 74–78
    scouting for, 104–7
    and seeing around blind spots, 84–87
    and sharing wisdom/responsibility, 92–97
    tickling as a point of, 121–22
consequences, 30, 70
contingencies
    achieving behavior modifications with, 68
    and behavioral recipes, 37
    building resilience by changing, 80
    and changing the environment, 60
    and mealtime/food preferences, 68, 69
    and vocabulary of behavioral science, 30
continuous improvement, 41
Corinthians, letter to (biblical), 110
corporal punishment, 68, 98
COVID-19 pandemic and vaccines, 22, 23, 143–44, 149
cues (stimulus control), 35
culture, family, 81, 144, 146–47

cusps, behavioral, 60–64
Czekalski, Sara, 100

dangerous habits, 46–47
dangers faced by people with autism, 125–26
deference, 87–91
dentist visits, 83–84
detachment, sense of, 121
diagnosis of autism, 116–17
diapers, dirty, 126
differences, honoring, 72
difficulties, learning to tolerate, 134
dignity, treating children with, 144
disease model of medicine, 27–28
disgust, power of, 126–27
do-no-harm oath, 47
Down syndrome, 82, 95
Ducharme, Joseph, 134
Dunst, Carl, 139

Earhart, Amelia, 57
early intervention programs, 48, 123
eating inedible things (pica), 131
echolalia, 62
Edelen-Smith, Patricia, 61
emotions, 55–56, 118–24, 147
employment, 62–63, 142–44
Ennis-Cole, Demetria, 106
environments
    changing, 60–61, 63–64
    for learning, 40
envy, feelings of, 117
Ephron, Nora, 16
EPIC, 107
ethical standards/guidelines, 22–23, 27, 102–3
eugenics, 23

evidence-based treatment, 36–43
evolutionary biology, 23
exit strategies from services, 104
experimental psychology/psychologists, 18, 21–22, 26
experiments in research, 103
extinction, 31
extinguishing behaviors, 45–47
eye contact, challenge of, 128–29, 137–38

families of children with autism
    access to care, 49
    attending to bids for connection, 139–40
    and building resilience in children, 80–81
    and child abuse/neglect, 100–101
    as collaborators and allies, 109
    and communication of children, 98–99
    connecting within, 74–78, 98–101, 119, 124, 139–40
    criticisms of, 90
    dealing with uncertainty, 149
    disgust/rejection experienced by, 127
    emotional awareness in, 120
    and good vs. good enough, 142–45
    and joyful interactions, 114
    and limited resources, 93–94, 101, 144
    and making meaning, 150
    and mealtime/food preferences, 64–65
    and "normal" lives, 123
    and other children in families, 99–100
    providers' relationships with, 26
    and reciprocity, 74–78
    resilience of, 122–23
    resource/energy management in, 130
    role of emotions in, 118–19
    routines of, 119
    and siblings, 75–76, 99–100, 136–37

values and cultures of, 81, 90, 144, 146–47
fear, 55, 124, 141
feelings, 55–56
Fifita, Ruha, 140
1st Corinthians, 13:4-8, 110
fixations, 45–47
flexibility in treatments, 42
focused therapies, 48–49, 51–52
focusing, difficulties with, 33–34
food preferences, 64–70
force-feeding, 65–66
forcing behaviors on children, 137–38
Fox, Matthew, 47
friends
    and fostering connections with reciprocity, 74–78
    and learning/growth opportunities, 72
    of school children, 75
    unsolicited opinions offered by, 117–18
Frost, Lori, 131
funding for autism services, 94

Garden, Regan, 118–19
gender identity/expression, fluidity in, 117
generalization, 71
Gerhardt, Peter, 146
Gill, Barbara, 147
Goldiamond, Israel, 118, 119
good and good enough, discerning between, 142–45
grade fluctuations, 34
gradual exposure with interventions, 66
Grandin, Temple, 118
Great Society programs of Lyndon B. Johnson, 21
Guðmundsdóttir, Kristin, 59
guilt, parents' feelings of, 116, 122

halcyon attitude, 55, 150–51

halitosis, 127
Hamby, Deborah, 139
Harris, Sandra, 100
hazardous attitudes, 53–54
health professionals, 44–45
helplessness, 79
heroism, 144
Higashida, Naoki, 118, 132
Hippocratic oath, 47
history of research into autism, 23–24
HIV research, 22
Ho, David, 22
hope, allowing room for, 150
humanity
    honoring, 148
    responding to children with autism with, 144
Hurston, Zora Neale, 110
hygiene, personal, 126–27

idiomatic speech, 60
ignorance of autism, 21
imitation
    and behavioral cusps, 61–62
    and one-on-one learning, 58
    and opportunities for connection, 105–6
    teaching, 32–33, 38–39, 61–62
impulsive attitudes, 53, 54
independence, 79, 81
inspiration and science, 151
institutionalization of children with autism, 10, 25, 26, 135
instructions, following, 134
insurance companies, 49
intelligence of children with autism, 135
intention/intentions, 92–94, 108–9, 113
interests of children

intense levels of, 45–47
  respecting/leveraging, 62, 71–72

interventions, behavioral
  and behavioral cusps, 61
  and behavioral science, 28
  comprehensive treatment programs, 48–49
  and continual adjustments, 42
  contrasted with medical pathologies, 27–28
  difficulty of, 32
  and early attitudes toward autism, 10
  early intervention programs, 48, 123
  emergence of better, 25
  flexibility in, 42
  focused therapies, 48–49, 51–52
  gradual exposure with, 66
  intentions underlying, 92–94
  and marketplace of autism services, 26
  parents' involvement in plans for, 34–35
  social affection embedded in, 69
  wraparound plans, 50–52
intimidation experienced by parents, 96–97
invulnerable attitudes, 54
isolation, feelings of, 11, 76, 82, 125, 127, 131

jealousy, 117
job support, 62–63
Johnson, Lyndon B., 21
joy, 112–15, 118, 124

Keenan, Mickey, 27
kingfishers, 151
Kingsley, Emily Perl, 95
Koegel, Lynn, 34, 66
Koegel, Robert, 25, 34, 66

Lao Tzu, 78

Larousse Gastronomie (Montagne), 37
Latham, Glenn, 42, 129
law enforcement, connecting with, 125–26
Leaf, Ron, 38
learning, 20–72
    and behavior analysis/applied behavior analysis, 20
    continuous, 134–35, 151
    and early research on autism, 25
    environments for, 40
    goals, 50
    historical attitudes toward, 20
    learning to learn, 64–72
    motivation's role in, 20
    in natural environments of childhood, 105
    from one another, 82–84
    one-on-one, 57–58
    positive perceptions of, 71
    power of, 12–13
    reinforcing behavior with food, 70
    and relearning, 123
    shaping and responsiveness to, 138–39
LeBlanc, Judy, 114
Lekotek, 119–20
Lentine, Scott, 104
Let Me Hear Your Voice (Maurice), 25
Long, Judith Steven, 25
Louis, Don, 63
Lovaas, O. Ivar, 25–26
love and loving, 110–51
    Apostle Paul's words on, 110
    and attention, 128–34
    dark side of, 115–24
    and deeper connections, 134–40
    and joy, 14, 112–15
    learning to love, 125–28

and making meaning, 140–48
  power of, 14
  and showing affection, 135
Luke (biblical), 87
Lutzker, John, 86, 98–99, 100, 122

macho attitudes, 54
marginalized communities, 111
marketplace for autism services, 26–28, 49
Matisse, Henri, 84
Maurice, Catherine, 25–26, 30
McAnulty, Dara, 149
McDuff, Greg, 133
McEachin, John, 38
McGee, Gail, 105
mealtime and food preferences, 64–70
meaning making, 140–48, 150
Mediterranean Sea, 150
Mees, Hayden, 24
meetings with school professionals, 88–91, 96–97
menstruation, 147
mentors, 39
misunderstandings about people with autism, historic, 135
modeling behaviors, 69
momentum, harnessing, 134
Morton, Thomas, 108
motherhood, 146
motivation, 20

negative reinforcement, 71
noises and sensory overwhelm, 132

obstetrics, 23
odors, 127–28
one-on-one learning, 57–58
Openden, Daniel, 66
open-mindedness, 52

operant psychology, 21
origins of autism, 115
O'Rourke, Nicolas, 115
Oxford University Hospitals, 142

Parenthood (film), 147
parents of children with autism
   and adolescent/adult children, 107
   advocacy role of, 97
   alliances and communities of, 94–95
   AM radio metaphor for journey of, 42
   awareness of attitudes, 52–55
   and behavioral science, 29
   blaming one another, 127
   blind spots of, 86–87
   and building resilience in children, 80–81
   challenges faced by, 114–24
   complex situations faced by, 18
   and difficulty of securing services for children, 89–90
   and early attitudes toward autism, 10
   and early research on autism, 25
   and emergence of formal treatment options, 10
   expertise/skills of, 59
   fears and worries of, 115–16, 141
   and feelings of guilt, 116, 122
   goals of, 83, 84
   instincts of, 92
   intimidation experienced by, 96–97
   and joyful interactions, 112–13
   and judgmental strangers, 56, 57
   lack of sense of urgency, 10–11
   love for children, 43
   meetings with school professionals, 88–91, 96–97
   partnerships with professionals, 82–84
   professionals deferring to, 87–91

resentment and envy experienced by, 117
　　responsiveness of, 139
　　risk of dependency on professionals, 97
　　and science of behavior change, 35–36, 42
　　and sense of detachment, 121
　　and shame, 43
　　stormy relationships with children, 129–30
　　and treatment plans for children, 34–35
　　and unsolicited opinions of others, 117–18
　　and whole-system thinking, 45–47
　　wisdom shared by other, 94–97
Parent-to-Parent (peer group), 15, 104
Park, Clara Claiborne, 98, 135–36
Pasteur, Louis, 26
Paul (biblical), 110
Penzey's Spices, 64
Perelson, Alan, 22
perseverations, 45
perspectives/attitudes, importance of, 52–55, 84–87
physical activity levels, improving, 145–46
pica (eating inedible things), 131
picky eatings, 64–70
play, 112–13, 132–33, 136–37
police departments, connecting with, 125–26
Potucek, Jessica, 79
"power" (term), 17
The Power of Positive Parenting (Latham), 129
preferences of children, 70–71, 79–80
preferred activities (potential reinforcers), 35
Princeton Child Development Institute, 133
privacy of children and families, 19
problem behaviors, 24–25
professionals in autism field
　　and advocacy role of parents/caregivers, 97
　　attachment to clients, 121

awareness of attitudes, 52–55
blind spots of, 85–86, 87
bumpy starts with, 103
as collaborators and allies, 108
comprehensive treatment programs of, 48–49
deferring to parents, 87–91
disgust and rejection from, 127
ethical standards/guidelines, 27, 102–3
exit strategies from services of, 104
expertise/skills of, 58–59
families' relationships with, 26
inexperienced/unskilled, 39–42, 137–38
intentions of, 94, 120
and intentions underlying treatments, 92–94
and intimidation experienced by parents, 96–97
and joyful interactions, 112–13
parents as equals among, 87–91
parents' partnerships with, 82–84
and professional standards/credentials, 27, 101–4
and provision of basic care, 126
push back against developments in field, 11
sincere caring of, 120–21
wisdom shared by experienced, 94–97
See also behavior analysis/analysts
profit-based therapies, 26–29
progress, human, 150
prompts, external, 40
pronouns, 19
protecting people with autism, 125–26
Proust, Marcel, 82
pseudonyms, 19
punishing behavior, 24–25, 29, 68, 71, 123
punitive practices, 40, 67–68

The Reason I Jump (Higashida), 118, 132

reciprocity as means of fostering connections, 74–78
reforms in autism field, 10
"refrigerator mothers," 115
reinforcing behavior
    and expertise of behavior analysts, 36, 71
    with food, 70
    increasing parents' methods for, 70
    with joint activities, 113–14
    with joyful interactions, 112
    and joyful interactions, 113–14
    and mealtime/food preferences, 69–70
    power of, 33
    and timing of reinforcements, 35
    and vocabulary of behavioral science, 29–30
rejection, social, 126–27
relationships. See connecting and connections
research into autism, 10, 27, 49
resentment, feelings of, 117
resigned attitudes, 53, 54
resilience
    allowing room for, 150
    building, 78–81
    and coping with struggles, 134
    and early adulthood, 148
    of families of children with autism, 122–23
    importance of, 57
    thriving as goal of, 43
resistance, joy as act of, 115
responsiveness, 41, 139
resurgence of behaviors, 31–33
retraining children, 40
Rilke, Rainer Maria, 55
Risley, Todd, 24
Rivera, Geraldo, 25
Rogers, Fred, 125

Rolfe, Randall Colton, 92
Rosales-Ruiz, Jesus, 55, 60, 66
running away, 131, 132

Sackett, David, 142

school
    advantages/disadvantages of learning in, 58
    difficulty with focusing in, 33–34
    and grade fluctuations, 34
    meetings with school professionals, 88–91, 96–97
    and professionals deferring to parents, 88–90
    securing services for children in, 89–90
    specialized services offered by, 49

Schopenhauer, Arthur, 29

science
    of behavior change, 42 (see also behavior analysis/analysts)
    and ethical considerations, 22–23
    gray areas in understanding, 29
    and inspiration, 151
    and LBJ's Great Society programs, 21–22
    nature/limitations of, 22–23
    as process of discovery, 28
    progress inherent in, 28

"Science for Sale: But at What Price?" (Keenan), 27
scolding children, 31
seclusion, children's time in, 24
See Sam Run (Heinkel-Wolfe), 16
selective eaters, 64–70
self-harm, 131, 132
self-management, 35
self-monitoring attention, 34
sensory overwhelm, 132
sexuality, 128, 146
Shakur, Tupac, 115

shame, feelings of, 43, 127
shaping (technique), 137–39
Shaw, George Bernard, 36
shortcuts, risks associated with taking, 29
siblings, 75–76, 99–100, 136–37
The Siege (Park), 135
Sigurðardóttir, Gabriela, 59
Simmons, James Q., 25
skills, learning new, 37–38, 48, 131
Smith, Garnett, 61, 76–77
social affection, 69, 70
social cues, 129
social interactions/growth, 32
social media, 117
social skills, 77
sound, sensitivities to, 101–2
spanking, 68, 98
special education programs, 88–89, 91
speech therapy, 89
Stein, Gertrude, 84
stigma associated with autism, 21
stimulus control, 71
stimulus discrimination, 71
strangers
    judgmental, 56
    unsolicited opinions offered by, 117–18
strength, building personal, 78–81
struggles
    coping with, 134
    value of, 78–79
stuffed animals, reliance on, 80
substitutions made in treatments, 41
suffering, 57
support for important tasks, building, 133–34
sustainability, 47–52

teachers, 44–45
Team Help, 106–7
technology of behavioral science, 29
Teresa, Mother, 74, 128
therapy compared to science of behavior analysis, 42
time outs, 68
toileting, 126–27
Tolstoy, Leo, 134
toys used in therapeutic interventions, 93–94
transitions, difficulties with, 133
treatment centers, staff in, 94
Trivette, Carol, 139

uncertainty, dealing with, 149
university labs, 49
University of North Texas Press, 16
University of Washington, 24

values of families, 81, 90, 144, 146–47
video clips, instructiveness of, 113
vulnerability of people with autism, 125–26

"Welcome to Holland" (Kingsley), 95
Whitman, Walt, 52
whole-system thinking, 44–47, 142
Williams, Donna, 118
Willis, Jamaun, 147
wisdom, sharing, 94–97, 108
Wolf, Montrose, 24, 120
The Wonderful Wizard of Oz (Baum), 9, 12
working hard, value of, 78–79
A Work in Progress (Leaf and McEachin), 38, 39
Worling, David, 134
wraparound plans, 50–52

You've Got Mail (film), 15–16
Yummy Starts, 66–70

www.ingramcontent.com/pod-product-compliance
Lightning Source LLC
Chambersburg PA
CBHW050522100526
44581CB00002B/77